Aren't We Sioux Enough?

By Eunice Davidson
"Wicanhpiwastewin"
(Good Star Woman)

"I believe much trouble would be saved if we opened our hearts more. I will tell you in my way how the Indian Sees things. The white man has more words to tell you how they look to him, but it does not require many words to speak the truth."

Chief Joseph
(Hin-mah-too-yah-lat-kekt) Nez Perce
1840-1904

DEDICATION

In Loving Memory
"Grant Michael Davidson, Love of our Life"

1992-2011

This Book is dedicated to our Grandson "Grant Davidson" in his loving memory who loved to play hockey though his Elementary and High school years and had dreams of playing for the Fighting Sioux Hockey team at the University of North Dakota. The day before his passing we had a visit; he asked me "Grandma, Do you think we will save the name and logo at the University?" I told him we're trying. He said "don't ever give up Grandma, that name and logo gives me pride."

Also dedicated, two more warriors who have journeyed on to the Spirit World and who supported and had pride in the University of North Dakota using our name and image. *Alex Yankton* who was a Committee member from Spirit Lake, and *Tom Iron* who was a Veteran and Elder from Standing Rock.

TABLE OF CONTENTS

Acknowledgements	Page 10
Author's Note	Page 13
History Repeats Itself	Page 14
Introduction by Frank Burggraf	Page 18
Chapter 1: Our Early Years	Page 27
Chapter 2: The Awakening	Page 33
Chapter 3: What Could Or Should We Do?	Page 39
Chapter 4: Put Into Motion	Page 48
Chapter 5: Efforts to Bring About a Vote	Page 53
Chapter 6: Anger and Confusion	Page 62
Chapter 7: The Next Step, Another Ambush	Page 72
Chapter 8: Things Are Becoming Clear	Page 78
Chapter 9: Continuing the Fight	Page 88
Chapter 10: A New Strategy Is Needed	Page 97
Chapter 11: Fall Out Through Hot Air	Page 106
Chapter 12: A Break With Some History	Page 115
Chapter 13: The Fog Begins to Lift	Page 127
Chapter 14: The Next Hurdle	Page 137
Chapter 15: It Never Stops	Page 156
Chapter 16: It Never Seems to Change	Page 171
Chapter 17: North Dakotans Speak	Page 183
Chapter 18: The Conclusion and Some of My Thoughts and Opinions	Page 197
Chapter 19: They Just Won't Let It Go	Page 206
The Fighting Sioux Spirit; A Special Note	Page 211
References	Page 212

ACKNOWLEDGEMENTS

A Special Thanks to so Many Who Supported this effort and who tried to help save "The Fighting Sioux Name and Logo...

First of all the love of my family:

My husband who stood by me through the many travels, and always ready to do what he could to help, my children Davy, Joy, Lisa, Lance, and my grandchildren, Melissa, Demery, Destiny and our Great Granddaughter Maliyah. To my many relatives on the Spirit Lake Nation & Standing Rock...

Our Committee for Understanding and Respect Members...

John Chaske, Joseph Lawrence, Frank Black Cloud, Renita Delorme, Lavonne Alberts.

And to the 67% of Spirit Lake Members Who Voted in Support.

Attorney's Reed Soderstrom, Gordon Caldis, Stephen Behm, and Jerry Rice

Standing Rock Members, Archie Foolbear, Bobby & Diane Gates, Antoine American Horse, and many more including the 1004 who signed the petition to have a vote on Standing Rock.

The Alumni who stood with us...

Frank Burggraf, Sean Johnson, Kris Casement, Pam Brekke, Tammy Washburn, Bennett Brien, Terry Brien, Lisa Carney, Bill LeCaine, Gaylord Peltier, Ella Black Cloud Gail Martinson, Marilyn Schoenberg, Don Barcome, Tim Heise, Charles Tuttle and Bella his dog. The Citizens of North Dakota, Minnesota, and so many other fans from around the Country. Your fortitude and stamina to stand with us in the cold, heat, and rain for the petition signings. Will forever be grateful for all your help.

Thank you to Amanda Brinkley for her Design work.

Thank you to so many who made a donation to our Fighting Sioux fundraiser it was very much appreciated.

Special thanks to Henry & Kathe Boucha for all their help with publishing this book for their support and friendship...

Author's Note

As we reflect back on the events of the past 7 years of defending the Fighting Sioux nickname at the University of North Dakota (UND), to say that the time has been challenging is an understatement. Those who oppose the Fighting Sioux nickname at UND have proven to be a formidable group. Although small in number, their tactics have been less than honorable yet predictable. Many have asked why fight them? Because the name was given by our forefathers and we are to honor their gift.

There were times when my strength and resolve have been tested but the spirit that energizes the Symbol at UND by my forefathers and my grandmother has lifted my spirits and put me back on the good trail of Truth and Principle.

I want to express my heartfelt thanks to the many friends of the Fighting Sioux who have come to the aid of the Sioux fighting to retain the Fighting Sioux Symbol and 80 years of tradition at UND. There are thousands of you who have reached out to David and me and others and you are too many to list, but you know who you are and I thank you for your convictions, support, contributions and energy. The fight must continue and I shall continue to raise my voice in defense of the Fighting Sioux Symbol at UND.

I would like to thank all of you who came out in the frigid cold , the hot summer sun and stepped up to sign the petitions, following the Sioux Pride RV and those who supported the efforts to defend the gift given to UND by our forefathers and the right to carry our great Sioux name at UND.

History Repeats Itself

You know how you wake up some mornings and hear on the news some stupid story and think to yourself, "That doesn't make sense! But oh well, somebody just needs to justify their existence," and you go about your normal routine and think no more of it.

But, as time goes by *that stupid story comes back to haunt you!* Such is the story here in North Dakota over the Fighting Sioux name and symbol, and I'm sure in other states as well.

The world is made up of mostly wonderful and honorable people. They are husbands, wives, career men and women, laborers, bankers, stay-at-home parents and many others. They go about their days minding their own business and they try to stay out of other people's business. They have no desire to put themselves in the spotlight. They express their opinions to friends and family, but not to the world. But like everyone they have issues they feel passionate about.

There are those also who make their living from turmoil and there are those who can only justify taking up space on this earth by creating trouble. And then the *most dangerous*, those who have a piece of paper (DIPLOMA) proclaiming they are so smart that GOD must get off his throne because it now belongs to them.

It is impossible for me to relate to this last group, because I am a mere mortal. I do not have the gift of reading minds. I cannot tell the future. I do not have the ability to tell you what you feel; even if you don't know you feel it yourself. I cannot go into a geographical area that I know nothing about and instantly know the answers to bring about utopia.

Don't get me wrong, I have a great deal of respect for people who have sought and acquired the knowledge to earn a diploma in whatever field they have chosen. They are the majority of college graduates in the past and present world. They use that knowledge to give, not to dominate. At present I am among those in pursuit of the education needed for that piece of paper, but it is the knowledge I seek.

But sadly there are those who have cheapened the value of the diploma, by buying them or cheating to get them or they may even fulfilled all requirements, but they use those diplomas to legitimize what they already believe – *that they are gods and they are going to save the world whether you like it or not*!

This is the group I believe we dealt with in North Dakota. This is my own *opinion,* but it is based on facts and how I perceived those facts. I was totally unaware of what the future had in store for me and our committee and tribal members - what obstacles and deceit awaited us just around the corner.

In this book I will present the facts and what my thoughts were at those times as I learned them and let you make up your own mind, if you agree or not. I will be as objective as possible, but I do feel a passion for this issue. I will present fact as fact and opinion as opinion. I will not give you what I heard so much as what I have witnessed. I will not tell you the rumors I've heard or try to destroy people's reputations through lies. I will tell you where to find the *news stories* and when I say that I heard it said, there will be witnesses to it. I will not ask you just to take my word for it.

Although we have not found a smoking gun, we believe the evidence will show a conspiracy did exist and it will indicate just who the conspirators are. It will suggest the handful of Native Americans agitators who believe they are using the elite to get rid of names and images are in fact being used by those elites to get what they want, which I believe is "THE TOTAL ASSIMILATION AND EVENTUAL DESTRUCTION OF INDIAN PRIDE AND TRUE HISTORY."

15

This story is not about a bunch of crybabies and whiners, but about our heritage and the fighting spirit our ancestors instilled in us. Although there is no comparison to the death and destruction our ancestors faced in 1850's to 1890's make no mistake the war has not ended and just as our ancestors fought overwhelming odds, we today find the same deceit and distortions in the elites practice of exterminating our very existence and true history.

The story is still in progress as I write and I am not sure how it will play out, but at the end I only ask you to make up your own mind.

If I offend anyone it is not my intention, I just want people who support Native American Indians and our Names and Imagery to know you are not alone out there, not just for historical reasons; the history of our Tribal Nation must never be forgotten.

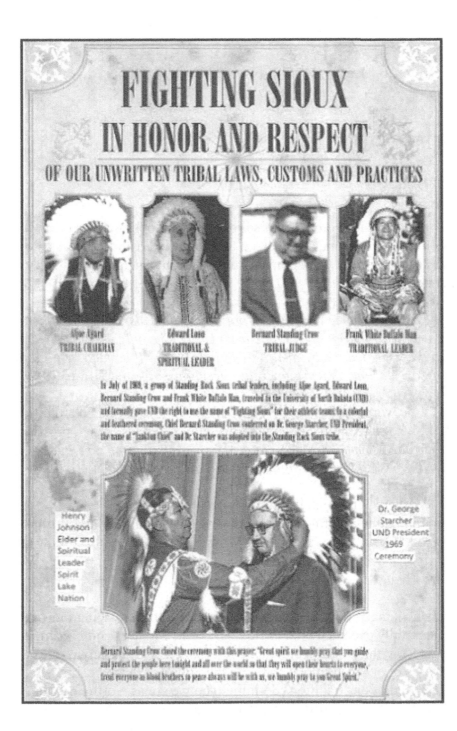

INTRODUCTION

Great traditions are born of solid leadership possessing a clear vision that enables men to walk on an untraveled path to success. 80 years is a long time. For some it is a lifetime, a generation that has spanned two ages.

"There will come a day when politically liberals will gather to remove the Fighting Sioux name from UND. The only way for UND to keep the name will be by the Sioux People who will have to bring it to the Federal Court under their religious rights." Tom Clifford 1984.

In the words of former UND president, Charles E. Kupchella, Ph.D., who stated in the closing of his letter to Myles Brand, president of the NCAA June 7th 2006, *"sometimes- even at some cost and some risk- it is best to stand up against injustice."*

As you read through the chronological order of the events surrounding the Fighting Sioux nickname debate, author and full-blooded Dakota Sioux, Good Star Woman, Eunice Davidson brings to you firsthand accounts of these telling events in her book "Aren't We Sioux Enough?"

I encourage you to keep a keen eye out for the low-lying indicators of a carefully executed plan to rid UND of its Fighting Sioux name. Targeted by those who were appointed (not elected) in public roles as stewards of our institutions and with the power of those positions, seized hold of our traditions defining who we are as North Dakotans. Ironically, this happened soon after the passing of two key stalwart figures that were pillars of UND and its storied history as the University of North Dakota Fighting Sioux.

In any fair debate there are two distinct and defined sides of the argument. Both sides have the opportunity to engage in critical conversations arguing their points. Although the Fighting Sioux issue could be coined as a political debate, <u>it was far from the arena of a fair debate</u>.

As you read through the book consider the following key points;

The actual people who gave the Fighting Sioux its name, were never allowed to be heard. The Fighting Sioux name was coined as "hostile and abusive" and now is a "racist" name. The very people represented by the Fighting Sioux name, were never included or invited to the table to discuss the issue with UND, the NCAA, or legislative individuals in North Dakota. This is a key point crucial to exposing the actions of the stewards of our state institutions trying to rid UND of its Fighting Sioux nickname.

Consider the fact that many former key leaders at UND were actually UND alumni and residents of North Dakota while the current UND administration never set foot in the Dakota Territory prior to applying for their current positions at UND.

Ralph Engelstad and Tom Clifford, were arguably some of the most visible and vocal supporters of the traditions at UND, along with many other UND alumni. For years they built UND to the highly respected institution it enjoys today. Only after the passing of these true legends of UND, does the opposition initiate its full court press on the Fighting Sioux name embracing the aid of the NCAA.

Where does the source of this dissention at UND originate? It comes from within the classrooms and shadows in the halls of UND. A handful of professors who have together, coerced to impose their political agenda and opinions onto the traditions of UND. For years the opposition has slowly crafted their agenda to remove the Fighting Sioux name from UND. The late president Tom Clifford spoke of that agenda and warned us to be watchful of them. As more people who thought this way gathered at UND, and were recruited for positions of power, they became emboldened to press forward with their agenda.

They crafted a well-orchestrated attack with complete media bias on their side to carry their water and control the message employing fear tactics and using deceptive words to create a fear in the people of North Dakota.

Hardly a fair playing field for a critical "debate" on a campus that openly states in its mission to be tolerant, accepting, civil, and promoting cultural diversity. The question that goes unanswered was, "Why the Sioux were never invited to a sit at the table?"

The Sioux voice is not being heard. Even though there is 80 years of documented approval for the Fighting Sioux name to be used at UND, the Dakota Sioux have never been allowed to speak or be heard. The Spirit Lake vote in the Agreement, even though by majority voting, has not been counted nor considered in this debate.

With the leadership of the most dynamic personality and influential president UND has ever known, Tom Clifford, a true UND Alumni warrior, no longer on the roster and in the line up, and UND benefactor Ralph Englestad off the playing field, it was an easy assault for those few in opposition who for whatever reason had an axe to grind with the Fighting Sioux name at UND.

Why is UND held to a different standard than the other 8 collegiate institutions who carry Native Imagery? Those schools only had to have one tribal consent to carry their moniker forward while UND was to produce two different tribes. How is it that an agreement was made with UND, the North Dakota State Board of Higher Education (SBoHE), and North Dakota by the Executive Branch of the NCAA following a lawsuit, which produced a Settlement Agreement? In that Agreement, UND had to obtain two tribal approvals to carry the Fighting Sioux name onto the athletic field. Standing Rock and Spirit Lake are both Sioux Tribes. Standing Rock is Lakota and has 2/3 of its nation in South Dakota, while Spirit Lake is mainly Dakota and is sovereign to North Dakota. Standing Rock never participated in the vote. Spirit Lake (which is Dakota Sioux) voted and by a 2/3, majority approved the use of the name at UND. Why is Spirit Lake's voice not heard?

They raised the hostile and abusive challenge as the reason to retire the Fighting Sioux name and move on, many picked up the montage without merit even when it was proven to be false claims. *"It is time to move on. We cannot hurt the student athlete at UND,"* stated the president of the UND Alumni Foundation after exerting no effort to defend Sioux Pride. The alumni as a group was never polled or included in that decision to move on. Instead, it was decided by a few in a closed door room. Really? Why?

We have 80 years of use without any conflict that would *warrant* "moving on". This was the real first cut at the Achilles heel to strip UND of the Fighting Sioux nickname and demonstrates and exposes that low-lying agenda of removing the nickname.

After it was conclusively determined not to be "hostile and abusive" for UND to carry the Fighting Sioux name and a state law enacted by the people of North Dakota, the opposition quickly shifted to their new claim that *"No one will play us because of our name, the sanctions hurt UND"* stated the Athletic Director at UND. Stating this even though UND had just won the Western Collegiate Hockey Association (WCHA) final 5 as the Fighting Sioux and moved to NCAA post season play as just North Dakota and made it to the NCAA Frozen 4.

The citizens of North Dakota exercise their state rights as citizens of this country and move their legislators to action to make it "The Law". UND shall be known as The Fighting Sioux.

What is the response of the NCAA and the opposition? The NCAA slapped UND with "minimal" sanctions in NCAA post -season play and the opposition distorts those sanctions.

"Why"? Because the public institution of the state of North Dakota, which bears the historical ties to the indigenous people of the plains, the "Sioux", and the citizens exercised their rights as North Dakotans. The NCAA, a non-profit organization which was created to protect the student athlete from injury or abuse, is the one leading the charge against UND student athletes. The opposition bans the use of Native American names, imagery and mascots at public schools as though they own those entities as well as the names and images. This movement runs across the country in the same venue (Public Schools). These environments promote civility, tolerance, acceptance and cultural diversity. "Really"? They don't promote it, they control it.

21

What is the definition of racism? Are not the actions of the NCAA acts of racism? Would this statement of schools not playing UND because of its name be considered a racist statement? For a school to openly declare that they will not play another team because of its name or logo, especially after 50 years of rivalry and competition, shouldn't that statement be challenged as a racist statement? What is even more puzzling is those schools carry names that are native names.

What about the other eight institutions that carry native names and images? Isn't that discrimination to allow some the approval and others not? "Why is UND held to two Tribes for approval while the others are only needed one Tribe to agree its namesakes use"?

The Courts seal the documents surrounding the 2006 lawsuit and the NCAA. The questions have to be asked: "Why are those documents sealed? What is in them that require them to be sealed? Is this not public information?"

Some might think that maybe they are Custer's long lost cousins having returned and are seeking revenge against the Sioux. Some may even say, it is other native tribes gathering to defeat the Sioux and remove their name. Regardless of who "They" are, what Good Star Woman, Eunice Davidson brings out in her book "Aren't We Sioux Enough" is the truth behind those in power and their agenda to rid UND of its pride, honor and traditions known as Sioux Pride by its athletic alumni and generations of student body alumni who have embraced the gift to UND generations ago by Sioux tribal elders. But you will not read this information in the media even though they were in the stands during the debate.

The Fighting Sioux name is a great name for a great institution in a great state filled with great people from all walks of life. It has over 80 years of proof and evidence on its side to demonstrate this strong tradition. North Dakota has history with the Sioux people. They are as much a part of this state and country as anyone and enjoy the freedoms and rights afforded all of us by the founding documents.

The Sioux gave UND the Fighting Sioux name. It has been made moralistically right by the sacred Pipe Ceremony in 1969. It has been given numerous times by the Sioux over the years by ceremonies like the flag raising ceremony at the Ralph (2008). The Flag Raising

22

Ceremony at the Ralph where both Standing Rock and Spirit Lake Nations flags were raised at Ralph Engelstad Arena (REA) on the University of North Dakota campus. The Fighting Sioux name was referenced numerous times in the ceremony. If there were an issue of the use of the Fighting Sioux name and logo, would the Sioux have shown up to perform the Flag Raising Ceremony?

Yet, when asked to vote again, Standing Rock's tribal leaders prevented a vote from happening at the nation of Standing Rock. Why?

Spirit Lake voted overwhelmingly to keep the name at UND but their vote has been silenced.

But consider this:

By not allowing a vote. Standing Rock has never formally rescinded their tribal approval thereby honoring their forefather's gift to UND to use the Fighting Sioux name on the athletic field.

Yet in the end their agenda ran below the radar and covered up this fact and left the Spirit Lake vote uncounted. Under common law if you don't participate in a vote or cast a ballot you lose the opportunity to express your view. Your voice is not counted. But in this case, by Standing Rock not participating in the vote cancelled the Spirit Lakes overwhelming vote and silenced their voice. How is that right?

Where is the outcry for the fowl in the media? Where is the unbiased journalist reporting the story to public light?

The citizens of North Dakota moved their legislators to make it a state law that UND will be named the Fighting Sioux. Somehow, in a Republic where States have rights, a non- profit organization that was initially formed to protect the student athlete from abuse, and a state institution, who is funded by taxpayers of the State, collaborated to create a fear in the citizens to abolish the new law. This is significant in the debate.

In North Dakota, under the Corrupt Practices Law, it is unlawful for a state employee or public employee to lobby against or for an Initiated Measure. The University System in North Dakota is funded

23

by tax dollars. They are considered public employees. The Athletic Director placed the UND Athletic Head Coaches out front in a public statement against the IM and Repeal the Repeal Law. The Sioux petitioned the citizens of the State to make an amendment to the State Constitution to make the Fighting Sioux name use at UND protected by the State Constitution.

The Repeal the Repeal Law petition verbiage was voting YES to keep the Fighting Sioux name at UND and NO to retire the Fighting Sioux name at UND. In the 11th hour, the measure verbiage was changed to YES to retire the name and NO to keep the name. In any primary election, voter turnout is low. The issue that we face in a democracy is when we send ignorance into the voting booth. The issue faced in retaining the name is during the election was an overwhelming support of the petition of YES, keep the Fighting Sioux name at UND prior to the election, only to have the Attorney General of North Dakota change the verbiage on the measure to read YES to retire the name and NO to keep the name.

Changing the Measure verbiage prior to the vote created confusion in the voting booth. The amount of calls and emails that came in from across the state to the Committee for Understanding and Respect and Eunice with excitement about voting YES to keep the name demonstrates again, that the citizens of North Dakota were misled on an issue and measure that was close to their hearts.

Reading the pages of "Aren't We Sioux Enough?" you will walk alongside the Sioux who are fighting to keep the Fighting Sioux name at UND. You will follow the accounts of events of the fight to keep the Fighting Sioux nickname at UND. You will be armed with the truth behind the actions of deceitful hearts that employed verbal and written tactics to scare the good people of ND into retiring the Fighting Sioux name and tradition from UND.

If we keep the Fighting Sioux nickname we will have sanctions imposed on us. If we keep the Fighting Sioux nickname, no one will play us. We will not be accepted into a D1 conference. This was the message from the President and Athletic Director at UND. No one will allow us into his or her conference. Really?

What if we have evidence that all these accusations were false or embellished and became the montage of the opposition and the media sent that message out loud and clear. Yet, it was again a deceptive montage to scare the citizens of North Dakota to embrace retiring the nickname.

What it comes down to is simple. Reading the accounts of the battle to retain and defend the Fighting Sioux nickname is not about the opposition's accusations that are presented, as they are easily refuted and are without merit.

It is not about the actual accounts of hostility or abuse that have been proven false; it is about rights and opinions. When a person's opinion trumps another person's right, we as a society are in trouble, where do we draw the line?

Consider this:

Minnesota and Wisconsin inferred that they would not play North Dakota in hockey if they came out of the dressing room as the Fighting Sioux. It would be interesting to know if they would carry the same policy if they ended up in the NCAA Championship game and had to face the Seminoles, Utes, Illini or other Universities that carry Native American names and images.

In closing… The NCAA and powers to be have stated it is ok for UND to go as North Dakota. Really? What is Dakota?

It is SIOUX!

One word: Hypocritical
"Aren't We Sioux Enough" exposes the agenda.

Bring it back! Enjoy the read.

Fighting Sioux Forever.

Go Sioux!

Frank Burggraf
Wambdi-Ohanko

CHAPTER 1: OUR EARLY YEARS

Now that I can look back, I was fortunate to be introduced to different cultures at a young age. Although they were mainly from the Native Americans, I did watch TV and saw the Brady Bunch, The Andy Griffin Show, Dick Van Dyke and others. There are many painful memories, but there are many wonderful memories to. Most of them are for a different story. I think you need a little background material on me and my family.

I was born into a family of Traditional (Dakota Sioux) and I am a full blood and my parents both spoke Dakota Sioux fluently and English was a second language. I only speak English, and I am trying to learn the Dakota language. I have memories of those early days with my parents, but most I am kind of foggy. I have good and foggy moments with my mother of whom I always felt the kindness, and caring love that she did give us when we were still living with her. My father, I don't have too many good memories of him and I won't go into that at this time.

At the age of six, two of my brothers and I were placed into a foster home on the Devils Lake Sioux Reservation, now known as Spirit Lake Nation. I stayed there for the next 11 years, except for the one school year I attended the Flandreau Indian Boarding School. My two other brothers were placed in a foster home that happened to be the brother of my foster father and the sister of my foster mother. I also met my future husband there (a full blood Norwegian). The year was 1957 and it was one of the most painful times of my life.

I was too young to understand what was happening, I just saw all these people coming into our home. Who were these strange white people? What did they want? I was scared and crying, but as I had done before, I was trying to protect my 4 younger brothers. I was 6 years old and had taken on a mother roll for my siblings. We were eventually loaded up and hauled away, and I cried for my mother and father for many years to come. Two of my brothers and I were then placed at the foster home of Rose and Max Jetty. It was some time before I knew where my other two brothers were.

My foster parents were wonderful people and we came to look upon them as (we called them Grandma and Grandpa) a part of my family that would be forever in my heart. Grandpa Jetty was a mixed blood Dakota Sioux and spoke Dakota, French Canadian, English and Grandma Rose was a mixed blood French Canadian, Chippewa, Cree, who spoke French Canadian and English, why I mention this will become clear later. Over the years the Jetty's had taken in many foster children, most for short periods of time (most were Sioux). Three other kids were there when we arrived and we all grew up together. They were also full blood Sioux.

The Jetty's owned a small farm with 7 to 8 milk cows, we had a large garden about 3 acres, pigs, chickens and a team of horses. We were basically self-sufficient on the farm. We were required to pitch in with the work which taught us work ethics. They were far from being rich in money, but extremely rich in spirit. At the time we thought they were hard on us. I was baptize Episcopal at birth, but had to change to Catholic with no say in it, because of Rose. Every year for Lent, we were on our knees for 40 nights, saying the rosary. Also because of that and the nuns, I came to fear God, not love him. That has changed and I thank God every day now.

Once a week they would bring the cream into town, to the creamery. They would get about $25.00 to $30.00 dollars for a 5 gal can. That was spending money for the week. There was a lot of work that went into that money. We would have to get up around 6 AM to get the cows. Then we would milk them by hand and again in the evening. For those of you who have lived on a small farm and were not fortunate to have an electric cream separator, you will know about the hand crank. For us girls we had to wash all those darn disks. It was worse than doing dishes.

That spending money got us to the drive-in theater a couple times a month, in the 50's and 60's there were a lot of western movies, many cowboy and Indian movies. Once in a while there would be a lone Indian who might be a hero. The majority would have the Indians running around yelling and screaming. When they attacked they would set themselves up like ducks in a shooting gallery. Not a very flattering picture and not very accurate either.

Alcohol played a part in how we got to the foster home and it was present in our new home and for many years to come. My foster brother who is much older didn't drink that often (maybe once a month) but when he did WATCH OUT. The frequency increased over the years. Grandpa maybe 3 or 4 times a year, but he was a passive drinker, grandma didn't drink at all.

We wore hand-me-downs of hand-me-downs for cloths that were bought at Sister Pino's Catholic Thrift Store. For haircuts grandma placed a bowl on our heads and cut around it (not really but that is what our haircuts looked like), ha-ha. We rode the bus to school. There were but a few Non Natives at our school and they were quiet and polite. Students at school were mainly Sioux with some Chippewa and a few whites. Out of all those, it was just a handful of Sioux kids that made fun of us because of our clothing, hair and the most hurtful "your parents don't love you that's why you're where you're at (words that would stay with me for a very long time)!"

Rose and Max at times would start talking in French and us kids just knew they were talking about us (they weren't) they would carry on a lengthy conversation and we could tell they were upset about something. I know Rose loved us and the many other foster children (which were mainly Sioux) they had over the years, but at times she would be angry about something (not us) she would say " oh those dirty Sioux, there just no good" so I came to believe it.

The Jetty's didn't practice Native Spiritual customs, but many other customs, tradition and remedies were used almost daily. One such custom was every fall Rose would kill a skunk and hang the musk sack from a tree (some distance from the house) she said the scent keeps you healthy and we hardly ever got sick. Max did go to pow–wows, but no spiritual ceremonies that I know of.

29

So by the time I got married 1968 (sixteen and a half years old, just a kid) my belief of myself and my people was not very positive. My marriage didn't do much to improve that belief. My husband worked construction and usually didn't get home until late at night. If he wasn't working late, he was drinking and didn't get home until late. At the time I believed it was about me, instead of it being his problem. This went on for many years.

After getting married, occasionally I would have to go out to the farm and bring Rose to town for grocery or to pay bills. Max was getting too old to drive anymore and I was the only ride she could count on. But I would tell her how my life was going and her response was "you made your bed now lie in it." I felt I was doomed to misery for the rest of my life.

My days now were filled with, listing to music on the radio when I had spare time or watching soap operas on TV, when I wasn't working at the Lutheran Home taking care of the elderly. Waiting up for my husband to get home and usually arguing when he did get home.

My husband will tell you his story now:
I was born in 1944 and as my father told me, I cost $25.00. I don't know if kids are more valuable today as compared to 1944, but there sure is a hell of a difference in cost. I was the youngest of four. I have three sisters older than me.

My mother past away when I was a little over a year old and I have no memories of her. But my three sisters and I went to live with my grandmother in Washington State. At the age of seven, my father brought us back to North Dakota to live with him.

It was one hell of a culture shock. While in Washington State with my grandmother, we had TV and indoor plumbing, I was forced to bathe regular, three square meals a day and I had to go to school every day, including Sunday school. But almost immediately, I was cast in the life of Huckel Berry Fin, when we came back. We lived on the wrong side of the tracks literally. The railroad tracks were no more than 50 feet away from my bedroom that I shared with my dad. The old locomotives past our house about 8 times during the day and night with their lonesome whistle blowing when it crossed the highway at the end of the block. I actually miss that whistle to this day. But now,

30

we had an outdoor toilet, our drinking water was delivered once a week, we had no TV, I was going to school with holes in my cloths and we lived on mainly cereal and dried milk. I was staying out till 1 or 2 in the morning thru the summer and I also was getting into trouble.

By the age of 10, some of my closest friends were a Chippewa family that lived down the block from us. I seemed to relate more to them than other kids. I had white friends to, but they didn't like "those Indians". I never could understand that and I started spending more time with them than my white friends.

By the time I was 13, I had gotten into trouble with the law a number of times and it was suggested to my father that he get me out of town during the summer months or I would be heading for the reform school. Most of that trouble was with my white friends. The "West Side Gang" as we were called, or as I look at it today "The Little Rascals".

My sister had just married her first husband and I started spending my summers at the Jetty farm. My brother-in-law was 6 years older than me and I came to idolize him. I was like a little puppy dog following him around and when we would

visit with his friends, they were always asking "who's that little white kid following you?"

I grew up not knowing where I fit. The one thing I knew was "you tell me I can't, I'll show you I can" and that philosophy was to be with me for many years. It got me into trouble much of my life. But I felt more comfortable with Native Americans and my closest friendships were with Native Americans.

So I grew up not fitting with the normal white family (ma and pa with the kids) and I certainly did not pass for a Native American kid. But what it did teach me was to accept people for who they are not the color they are. I will always be grateful for that.

At 17, I joined the navy. I was able to make friends easy, regardless of race. But I had already learned if you want to have any

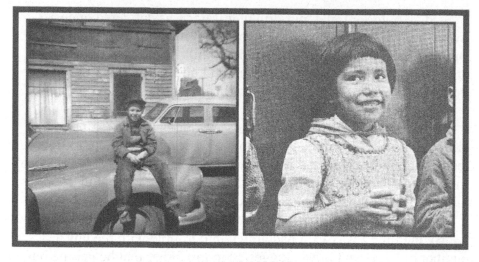

LEFT: Dave Davidson, 1954
RIGHT: Eunice Davidson

fun, drinking was where it was at. I got into trouble many times, but my work ability saved me. That went on for many years.

I brought that philosophy into my marriage and it almost destroyed it. Being married to a full blood and working mostly with Native Americans only strengthened my love for the Native American people.

The last twenty years, I have researched much of the history between Native Americans and the federal government. When it comes to the government, it is not by any means honorable. So much for our personal stories and now we go on to the book.

CHAPTER 2: THE AWAKENING

By the mid 1970's I had settled into married life. It was not what I expected. As a young lady, I had dreams of a little cottage with a white picket fence, and my husband cutting the lawn or tinkering around the house, and three or four kids, the family sitting down at the kitchen table, for breakfast, dinner and supper. After supper, we would sit around the table and talk about the day. I know that's a little much even for a dream, but it is exactly what I would have liked.

It was at this time when I was to hear about this University that called their team "The Fighting Sioux"! I loved to hang my clothes out on the line when it was summertime. I loved listening to music all the time, it always seemed to soothe me and let me have a good feeling. On that day when I heard the news sportscaster talking about the Fighting Sioux, I thought to myself isn't that something that a University who taught white people would want to be called by our name. At that time I knew I was a Sioux Indian, but had no idea of anything about my ancestors. I had never talked to hardly any of my relatives about our history, nor did I seem to want to find out anything at that time in my life. I suppose it had a lot to do with the stereotypical image I had seen and heard over the years. It was something I kept to myself and wasn't interested in hearing what was being said about Indians.

I had tried to find housing on the reservation when we were first married, but due to lack of housing on the reservation, we had to look for a home in Devils Lake. When we first moved into Devils Lake, in everything I did, I never noticed any racism or didn't pay attention to it.

But it was at this time something magical happened while hanging cloths on the line to dry, I knew now I would never have my little cottage. I loved my two children with all my heart, but felt there were no dreams left for me. I was just an Indian and not even well at that. There were times that I just wanted to run away and then reality would set in. I would not put my kids through what I had lived through. I did not have the self-confidence to think that I alone could provide for them. I FELT SO TRAPPED.

Then on that day, no different from any other, I was hanging cloths on the line with the radio turned up so I could hear the music, when all of a sudden "HERE COMES THE FIGTHING SIOUX" came blaring out of the radio. I don't remember if it was football or a hockey game, but as I turned toward the radio, they again said the UND Fighting Sioux are coming out. I knew that UND was the college in Grand Forks, but in my mind, I was not thinking about that. My mind was kind of racing; I knew that NDSU and UND were the big colleges of North Dakota. I knew from watching old movies that people love their college sports teams. I know you do not name something you love and respect after something you hate and have no respect for. Those people are cheering for the team they love and that team has chosen to honor my ancestors, the Fighting Sioux. I am a Sioux; I AM A FULL BLOOD SIOUX!

"Yeah" it sounds corny, but the day seemed a little brighter, I am not as my foster Grandmother said, we are not dirty Sioux (thinking of what my grandma's perception was about the Sioux) and people respect my ancestors (these were white people cheering). For those of you who have never lacked in self-confidence, self-esteem or pride in yourself or your people, you may not understand, but for those who have felt that empty feeling and had some insignificant thing happen to open your eyes, you know what I mean. There is a saying that I heard long ago, that I know to be true: "Self-esteem is not something we give our kids; it is something we take away." I had lost mine years ago and now some of it returned with what I just heard on the radio. Grandma was wrong when she said, "they're just no good" and I wondered was Grandma still carrying on a war that had long since been over. The vast majority of Chippewa and Sioux have buried the hatchet, but sadly there are a few that carry on the old hatred to this day.

When I was a young girl, we would go with Rose and Max to the Turtle Mountain Chippewa Reservation to visit Rose's relatives. It was clear that if you were Sioux, you had better be with Chippewa friends or trouble would find you. There is a population of Chippewa on our reservation and years ago they stayed mostly to themselves. But today we have pretty much bridged that old gap and many of our kids are even coming to Devils Lake and surrounding towns to work, and as I said, some still hold onto that old hatred.

It was about this time (mid 70's) that my son joined the squirt hockey team, and I was destined to become a hockey mom. My husband and son would usually watch UND hockey when it was televised, but I had no interest until now. We would only get about 4 or 6 games a year, at that time and we would sit down together and watch. We would get all excited when they won and we just knew it was thee officials when they lost. Ha... (We have to blame someone don't we?)

For the next 9 years, my car automatically found itself at the hockey arena in Devils Lake. Whether I would be going to the store or some other place, I would catch myself at the Bill Jerome or Burdick arena and realize it and say to myself "what the hell am I doing here?" My son developed a deep love for hockey and had a dream of playing for the Sioux. There is absolutely no doubt in my mind that this dream played a large part in my son graduating from high school. Every year his grades went up during hockey season, because he had to have good grades to play. That also became the case with my grandson.

There was much heartache attached to Devils Lake hockey. There were times I thought it was about race, but the same thing was happening to some white kids. From squirts through high school, some kids were left to bench warming while kids with lesser talent got more ice time during games. The heartaches drove many kids out of the hockey program at an early age, but my son and grandson's love of the game kept them going. It was difficult, but vital that we point out - this was happening to white kids also. I will never understand why this was and is still happening, but it has been a problem for years in Devils Lake, but that is for a different story.

My life continued to fall apart, my husband's drinking got worse and by now I had joined him. By 1991, the world was crashing down

35

around us. But I knew this was not about race it was about lifestyle. In 1991, when our marriage was about to end, we sought help and got into treatment. My husband likes to say "Dec. 7th, 1991 a day that will live in infamy". On that day we took our last drink. After we quit, bars had to open on Sunday's and hours had to be extended till 2 am, to make up for lost revenue. Haha.. Funny how things seem to appear that way!

Along with our new life came new challenges. My husband continued construction work and then was asked to work for the chemical abuse program on the Spirit Lake Reservation, which he did for a few years. He will always be grateful to the Tribe for that opportunity.

I went back to school at Little Hoop Community College and was voted student president. During this time a curious thing happened. While attending an American Indian Higher Education Consortium (AIHEC) conference in Bismarck, a group of us (about 26) all Native Americans with the exception of my husband who is full blood Norwegian and another white lady. Except for my husband we were all students and teachers. In one of the seminars the presenter was Native American, and at the beginning of his presentation, he asked us to take a piece of paper and write down the first three words that pop into our minds when he says this word. Don't think about it; just write the first three words? Then he said "INDIANS" and "Pass your papers forward."

At the end of his presentation, he informed us of the responses to his word "INDIANS". To a person, with the exception of my husband and the white lady, who wrote a hunter, a warrior, honorable, etc., the rest of us had written drunk, dirty, lazy, etc. He then said "Do you realize as educators, that is what you bring to our kids? And you expect them to feel pride in who they are?" I was amazed to realize, that although I learned that day while hanging clothes, "I am not a dirty Sioux", part of that old indoctrination was still there. I knew I had to change that and the opportunity came a few years later, by learning about my ancestors.

An elderly gentleman was brought to our reservation to do family histories. Paul Brill is a historian that retired from the Bureau of Indian Affairs (BIA). My daughter and her mother- in -law went to see him, and he told my daughter he has been dying to meet someone from our family. He said he felt like he was in the presence of royalty. We about fell over when we heard about it, but it intrigued me and I also went to see him. He told me about a little known chief in our family that actually should be held up there with Sitting Bull, Red Cloud and others – Inkpaduta.

This was in the mid 1990's. Mr. Brill gave us a family tree, which over the years I have been able to find many federal documents proving all my ancestors dating back to the late 1700's and early 1800's. I have official government documents which prove it. My husband, who has always had a love for the Native American people, was most interested in Inkpaduta. He has been able to paint a much different version of him than the white authors would have you believe.

In researching the history through the white man's writing, he has been able to reach a conclusion that most treaties were negotiated with honorable people in both communities. But the difference between the two communities was that when the Native American Chiefs and headmen put their mark too the treaty they smoked the Sacred Pipe. That was OUR BOND FOREVER, which we would honor forever, come what may. Some may call them fools for their trust we call them "Men of Honor".

The white community has many politicians who have no honor. What they say today can be changed tomorrow or soon as your back is turned. Unscrupulous White politicians, Indian Agents, Superintendents of Indian Affairs and trading post owners would seek out vulnerable Indians with lies or false promises. Most were mistakenly relying on interpreter's honesty which there was little, for they were paid by Politicians, a corrupt few Indians knowingly sold out their people for personal gain. And those were the ones corrupt politicians sought out. "The Treaty of Mendota, The Treaty of Traverse De Sioux, 1851" and the so called "Trader Papers" are means by which Alexander Ramsey stole almost everything from the Dakota and exemplify just one such case. (From; Source 33rd, Congress, "Report of the Commissioners").

That brings me to 2005 when I heard some stupid thing on the radio. The NCAA had adopted a policy that Native American names and imagery are hostile and abusive and will not be allowed.

I had no idea how much turmoil that stupid statement was going to cause in my life. I could not envision the confusion, anger, sleepless nights and the distortions and outright lies. The biased press hung right in there with it all. At times it felt like we were up against the whole world.

Now on to what I've experienced and truth of the story what has made us come to our conclusions?

Chapter 3:
What Could Or Should We Do...

It was in the summer of 2006 when I heard an announcement on the radio "THE NCAA HAS ADOPTED A POLICY TOWARD NATIVE AMERICAN NAMES AND IMAGERY". I wasn't even sure what it was all about. I just thought "somebody doesn't have anything to do, so they think up things to make themselves feel useful". I was still working on my family history and I had my job along with all the normal day to day living to deal with. That news report just didn't seem that important. I did not know then how much turmoil that bigoted statement was going to cause in my life.

I was unaware that what I now consider to be "evil forces" were conjuring up schemes to annihilate and erase my people from history. I can't tell what is in a person's mind, but I can't help but form opinions based on their actions. In this case, I believe their actions say a great deal. I hope you keep an open mind and form your own opinion.

I was ignorant of most of what was happening throughout the nation and world. I had a life, and it kept me quite busy. Between my grandchildren & grandsons' hockey, my job at a local grocery store on the reservation, my family tree, my education and my husband, there was little time left for national issues. We did find time however, to watch Sioux hockey together, when televised. We even attended a few games at the old arena and the new one. I never once felt the so-called hostility that has been thrown about by the media as commonplace.

At that time, I never believed the Fighting Sioux name and symbol would ever be removed.

The NCAA denied UND's request for exemption from the sanction policy that NCAA now has and a lawsuit resulted from it: November 11, 2006 The University, ND by and through the North Dakota State Board of Higher Education vs. The NCAA Lawsuit ND District Court *(case # 06-c-1333)

October 27, 2007 (Courtesy of the Joseph Marks and Grand Forks Herald): UND LAWSUIT: Settlement; The settlement states UND must win approval (from two tribes) for its nickname and logo or retire them by Nov. 30, 2010. *(Settlement/Agreement page 3 case # 06-c-1333)

But in the fall of 2007, the hammer had dropped! The NCAA and the North Dakota State Board of Higher Education had reached a court Settlement/Agreement with UND. I didn't even know there was a lawsuit at this time. But the Settlement/Agreement gave UND 3 years to get approval from the two Tribes of Sioux in North Dakota or lose the Fighting Sioux name and logo forever. I wondered at the time "where is all this coming from?".

I didn't know then, but later found out. It did not say UND must change the name and logo; it did not say the state of ND has no rights in this issue. What it did say the ND State Board of Education and UND had three years to SEEK and OBTAIN support from the two Sioux Tribes.

It finally sank in. The NCAA's policy was now that Native American names and imagery are "hostile and abusive". My question is to whom? Is it to the Native Americans? Then why would you not ask them? I don't mean just a small biased handful. Or is it they are ashamed of past political leaders (rightfully so) that signed treaties, only to violate them when it was politically or financially helpful? Are they not doing the same again?!!

Having lived through the late 60's and early 70's, seeing all the turmoil anti-Vietnam war demonstrations and the civil rights movement, drug use protests, I have been unfortunate to witness the birth of Political Correctness, where honesty, truth and common sense go out the window!

I do not lump the whole white race together as treacherous or deceitful. Just as the vast majority of Native Americans are honorable people, so are the vast majority of the white race, but I truly believed the saying "the only honest politician is a dead politician". I didn't know where this NCAA policy originated from, I can only assume, but the actions of the NCAA to this point and forward leave me with but one conclusion, which I will hold until later.

I would like to give a not-too-distant history lesson. In the 1970's AIM (American Indian Movement) garnered regional and national attention. I do not question the motives or the passion of the leaders of that movement, but I do question their tactics. I believe they did more harm than good. I share their anger and frustration of past injustices, but this was caused by some politicians and they had help in the Native community. It is not the people - but it is the politicians who are the guilty.

After AIM took over the Ft. Totten jail at Spirit Lake with an armed standoff, to this day it remains to be seen how it helped anything. God knows I have more reason to hate that jail than most, but I, as well as the majority of members I talked to, did not support their actions. Another example was their armed standoff at Wounded Knee, in which people died and one man's freedom has been taken away (possibly for life). It is totally up to Leonard Peltier as to whether or not he feels it was worth it. But in my opinion, the only thing I saw come out of it was that in both communities it fueled hatred and mistrust. Is that trust slowly fading away again?

I did have a respectful conversation with Mr. Peltier by phone in early 2009. He called and asked me how I could go against my tribal council, which I don't feel I had done. The Spirit Lake Tribal Council respects the people of Spirit Lake and did not wish to abuse their power by silencing the people. Once the people spoke, the Tribal Council respected the people and our traditional ways and stood with the people as is our tradition.

On the other hand, the Standing Rock Tribal Council has used their power to silence the people of Standing Rock and has dishonored our

41

sacred ceremonies. I would ask of Mr. Peltier, how can the Tribal Council go against its people and traditions?

I very much respect the people who are willing to put it all on the line for what they passionately believe in. But for those who say, their opinion is the only one that matters and are willing to go to any length to win, I do not. The end does not justify the means!

Getting back to the fall of 2007, there was quite a buzz around the reservation. Who wants to change it? Why do they want to change it? Where is this coming from? At my job I came into contact with many enrolled members. My family would joke, "Do you know everybody?" And the answer was "almost"!

Shortly after the announcement of the settlement on October 27, 2007, I called UND and asked what was going on and what could we do?

I did not hide the fact I was a supporter of the name and logo. Many members would ask me "what can we do?" I am no politician and I had no idea of what to do, so I called the University and told them who I was and wanted to talk with someone about what we were hearing on the radio. The lady on the phone said yes absolutely and put me touch with Phil Harmeson (Senior Associate to UND President Kupchella at UND) and I asked what could be done to help? He suggested I bring a group to UND and he would arrange a tour of the University and that a tribal vote would probably be the only thing to save it.

I did get a group together of about 20 of us. I don't remember the exact date, but it was early in 2008, and it was quite warm out. There was I and my son and his wife (another full blood) and a handful of other enrolled members. We traveled to Grand Forks (on our own dime). We did receive the tour and I must say we were treated with respect by UND staff and students everywhere we went. The only place we felt uncomfortable was at the Native American Center on campus, we did not know how the students knew we were in support of the name and logo, but as soon as we entered the building, they were asking us why we supported it. We were expecting to hear what a great college it is "because we knew so many had gone to school there for so many years", instead we felt a little intimidated, until my son

42

JOHN CHASKE WHO IS THE HEAD OF OUR COMMITTEE FOR
UNDERSTANDING AND RESPECT

went on the offense. He asked "why do you oppose it?" The main
reason they objected to the name and logo was "white students are
always asking us how we feel about it all the time". My son then
asked "AND?" Then we were expecting to hear some horror stories,
which they supplied none of. Then he asked "how many of you are
Sioux?" only one was part Sioux, out of about 11. The rest were from
other tribes. My son then asked "if you're not Sioux, why do you care?
It's not your heritage". No one shared any horror story of their
experiences, like the ones we had heard reports of and had been
suggested by some.

We were also somewhat surprised that the only place we went that
even mentioned the name and image was at the Native American
Center. We were there because of our support for the name, but not
one official brought the subject up and that seemed a little puzzling?

I must also add, I have been to UND many times; doing research,
attending seminars, concerts, and hockey games, before and after that
tour, and I have shopped in Grand Forks many, many times. I have
never felt the hostilities Grand Forks and UND have been accused of.

I have known of John Chaske for quite a few years, but never really got to know him well until one day my son told John that I was outraged by what was going on to the name and symbol. At that time, John had already formed a committee on Spirit Lake to see what they could do to help keep the name in place at the University. John contacted me and asked if I would join the committee. I told him I would be honored to. At that time I thought it shouldn't be an issue to have a vote here on Spirit Lake, and Standing Rock (yeah right!). Little did I know what turmoil it was going to cause!

Although I didn't see or read many news stories on the Fighting Sioux, the few I did read were not of a positive nature, but a few of us were busy talking to enrolled members in our daily activities. It was clear that there was overwhelming support from tribal members. You would see many of them wearing Fighting Sioux gear, sweatshirts, t-shirts, caps and other items.

John and others had already formed a committee and already had meetings by the time I joined. We shared the conversations we had with other enrolled members and came to believe that there was overwhelming support for the name and logo throughout the reservation. Just to be sure we decided to do a survey of members. If I remember right we surveyed close to 1200 members (young & old) and it was found out then only about 50 members did not approve or did not care about the issue. From that survey we knew we had the support of a majority of our tribal members. It was brought to our attention by members at Standing Rock that their flag was hanging inside the Ralph Engelstad Arena (REA), and thought it would be an honor to hang our tribal flag next to Standing Rock's. As a committee, we spoke to members, the elderly, spiritual leaders, and veterans, and by late summer all were in agreement. We would raise our Tribal flag alongside Standing Rocks at the Ralph Engelstad Arena (REA).

I was somewhat surprised to see the news story in the *(Courtesy of the Ryan Schuster and Grand Forks Herald) on September 13, 2008, of Chancellor Goetz feeling the need to shorten the deadline date. "WE CAN'T WAIT UNTIL NOVEMBER 2010": Our efforts were known. Why would he talk about shorting the deadline now, when there is positive movement on Spirit Lake?

By now, being involved in the process I was more aware and was reading the Herald daily. The news reports by now and those to come all seemed to have a negative overtone, down playing our efforts and over exposure to the opposition.

Sept. 27, 2008 *(Courtesy of Archie Ingorsoll and Grand Forks Herald): The REA to Display tribal flag; the story suggests majority of Sioux reject the name and logo and supporters are being used.

October 4th, 2008 *(Courtesy of Matt Cory and Grand Forks Herald): Attorney, State Board should take the Nickname case to trial. Gordon Caldis says under ND law we have one year to set aside the settlement and return to court. He is dismissed as a nice old man. I will come to know him very well later.

October 4th, 2008 *(Courtesy of Grand forks Herald): Spirit Lake group to head to Sunday's hockey game. The story totally minimizes the Flag raising ceremony.

Oct. 5, 2008 *(Courtesy of Chelscy Luger and Grand Forks Herald): Ceremony falsely suggests tribal support; the story gives one person's negative opinion. (An enrolled Chippewa from Turtle Mountains and UND staff)

Oct. 5, 2008 *(Courtesy of Donna Brown and Grand Forks Herald): Nickname issue pushes UND employee out the door. WHAT? After 15 years a person leaves to take a position at another college in a different city. It doesn't sound like being pushed out the door. It sounds more like a better job opportunity.

But these are the type of news stories to hit the newsstands from the Grand Forks Herald for the next few years.

On Oct. 5th, 2008, before the exhibition hockey game with Manitoba, our Tribal flag joined Standing Rock's Tribal flag above the ice at the Engelstad arena. It was a beautiful ceremony with over 100 enrolled members from Standing Rock and Spirit Lake attending. The Standing Rock members traveled 300 miles to be there and it is 100 miles from Spirit Lake, but the news coverage the next day was about the dozen or so protesters outside, most of whom weren't even Native

Americans and traveled maybe a mile or so, to be there. There were two other stories in the Herald that day, both negative.

Because there was no coverage of the ceremony that took place inside the REA, no one outside of those attending even knew it happened.

Oct. 9, 2008 *(Courtesy of Jennell Cole and Grand Forks Herald): ND Higher Education Board won't revive UND nickname lawsuit: The Board has decided that Mr. Caldis is wrong and that they have no grounds to return to court.

October 16th, 2008 * (Courtesy of Amy Philips and Grand Forks Herald): Amy Philips, Grand Forks, letter: Grand Forks Herald story, Professor Amy Phillips from UND, Letter: Nickname recalls a disrespectful era: The story suggest that the name and logo created "disrespect". She also states "I am a new employee at UND" I am proud to be here except for the name and image." *If she is new to the state how can she know anything about this issue or us? What has happened to the neutral position of the UND Administration? This is a total negative story on the name from a UND staffer.*

January 9th, 2009 *(Courtesy of Kevin Fee and Grand Forks Herald): Will Summit League decision speed things up?

Jan. 11, 2009 *(Courtesy of Mick Jacobs and Grand Forks Herald): It's time to drop UND nickname and logo, "It's clear now that UND name and logo cannot be saved" Summit league (just one of many deceitful tactics).

Feb. 10, 2009 *(Courtesy of Tu-Uyen Tran and Grand Forks Herald): Tribal members want nickname on the ballot: over half the story is why it shouldn't be.

We firmly believe because the people of Standing Rock and Spirit Lake have on many occasions over the years, demonstrated their support for the name and logo, the NCAA requirements should have been fulfilled when our tribal flag joined Standing Rock's. WE HAD NO IDEA WHAT WE WERE UP AGAINST! In the next weeks, months and years, we came to realize that we were not dealing with what we now feel were honorable people. The distorted stories in the

46

press, the constant changing of deadline, the new requirements, and the court battles (DISTRICT AND ND SUPREME COURT) all left us to draw but one conclusion - THERE WAS NEVER ANY INTENTION TO KEEP THE NAME AND LOGO, BUT A NEED TO BE ABLE TO BLAME THE SIOUX FOR THE CHANGE. This is something that was almost stated in court, both in Ramsey County District Court and in the North Dakota Supreme Court in Dec. 2009 and again in the early spring of 2010. I will elaborate on this later.

But here we were early 2009 and we still thought that the ND State Board of Education, the administration of UND, and the North Dakota news media were fighting alongside us. We believed we were all trying to save the name and logo and the villain was the NCAA.

CHAPTER 4: PUT INTO MOTION

I have gotten ahead of myself and need to back up just a bit.

Again, we are trying to relate the events as they happened, and what we felt at those times. It is very hard, knowing what we know now, but we will try to have you look through our eyes at those events as they happened.

Less than a year after the Settlement/Agreement was signed in District Court, in Grand Forks, although we did not know it at the time, some in the State Board of Higher Education members were working to change the agreement. As we found out later the agreement was signed on Oct. 27, 2007 and giving a time period till Nov.30, 2010. But on Sept. 13, 2008, Chancellor William Goetz statement in the Grand Forks Herald, "We can't wait until Nov. 30, 2010" as was agreed to in the settlement, I don't know if he just found out about our efforts on Spirit Lake or not, but all of a sudden, there seemed to be a rush to end the process?

Sept. 27, 2008, *Grand Forks Herald, The REA to display Tribal flags: Let the false accusation begin. From that day forward, supporter's honesty and integrity was challenged along with the Engelstad Foundation. Opponent's baseless accusation found their way into the media stories all the time and our correction were hardly ever mentioned, but the date was set for Oct. 5, 2008 for the flag raising ceremony.

*Grand Forks Herald Oct. 4, 2008, Spirit Lake group to head to Sunday's hockey game: In the story Standing Rock Tribal Chairman
48

Ron His Horse's Thunder said " UND is trying to make it appear as if it's honoring the tribes when that's not the case".

Now that is his opinion and not a fact, but the Herald does not state it that way. They did not seem to have any interest in truth. From that day forward the Herald prints accusations from opponents not bothering to fact check as to whether they can be backed up.

In early September of 2008, the truth is we had contacted the manager of the Ralph Engelstad Arena, not the other way around. We told him "we would" like the Spirit Lake Tribal flag to be raised there. He did not ask us, as the Herald stories suggested.

We asked, if it were possible and when would be the best time? He was quite happy, and said he would get back to us. It was worked out for Oct. 5th, 2008 and a lunch would be served for those who came early. We told him we were going to try to get a school bus for those who wished to go but had no transportation and would get him a list of how many.

Erich Longie, opposition leader on Spirit Lake and also President of the Four Winds Elementary School Board refused to allow the school to supply a bus for the elderly to make the trip, just as he had stopped UND athletes from coming to Four Winds School to encourage students to stay in school. We informed the REA of this and the manager said he would try to arrange a bus for the elderly. We gave him a list of how many from Spirit Lake were coming.

*Grand Forks Herald Oct. 5, 2008 "Viewpoint, Chelsey Luger; states that she is a proud member of the Turtle Mountain Band of Chippewa Indians. She also states her opinion as facts, she states that "UND and the REA are trying to silence the Sioux people", which is the exact opposite of the truth. There will be an injunction to stop the vote on Spirit Lake by a few tribal members "April 17, 2009" done by Erich Longie and numerous times from 2005 on "Ron His Horses Thunder, Standing Rock Chairman, the people will not get to vote".

Now it is my opinion that the ones who show disrespect and are dishonoring our people, our ancestors and traditions are Standing Rock Chairman and Erich Longie along with their co-hearts at UND.

Again, we are Sioux people who have pride in our ancestors and we asked to raise the tribal flag, it is not the other way around.

*Grand Forks Herald Oct 5, 2008 " Letter: Donna Brown, Moorhead, MN: (Another Turtle Mountain Chippewa and former UND staff) states her opinion as though it was fact, "that the tribal elders and veterans are being taken advantage of by the REA". Does she honestly believe that Sioux elders and veterans are too stupid to know what is good for them and are for sale? To stay at a job where you state you were so uncomfortable for 15 years, was her integrity for sale or is there some other motive behind her statement?

But the big day was here at last, it was October 5, 2008 and as I and my husband drove to Grand Forks along with my kids and grandchildren. I was quite excited and anxious. I had never been involved with anything like this before. As we walked into the REA, I noticed the handful of protesters off to the side and just shook my head.

But my heart pounded as the arena fell silent as Greg Holy Bull facilitated the event and I was so humbled. As I watched my people walk almost to center ice at the REA. There was Oliver in his traditional dance regalia led by honored veterans and elders with their war bonnets (the most respected in our traditions). The drum and singers were doing our traditional honor song as they walked out. A deep sense of pride flowed through me as my people spoke of the pride we felt, that such a proud University would choose to honor us, by naming their beloved University after our ancestors. 11,000 people were cheering and showing nothing but respect, as my people spoke. After the flag presentation and before the hockey game, the jumbo tron screen played the tribute to our ancestors as they do before every home game. Again a sense of pride ran through my veins. This was Oct. 5, 2008.

You can't imagine the disappointment and bewilderment I felt when I read and heard the news reports of the event; I wondered what event that reporter attended. It didn't seem to be the one I attended, because there were over one hundred enrolled members from Standing Rock and Spirit Lake there in support of UND and the Fighting Sioux, but a small handful of protesters outside got the coverage. Yet the news reports were all about the protesters. Statements from the

50

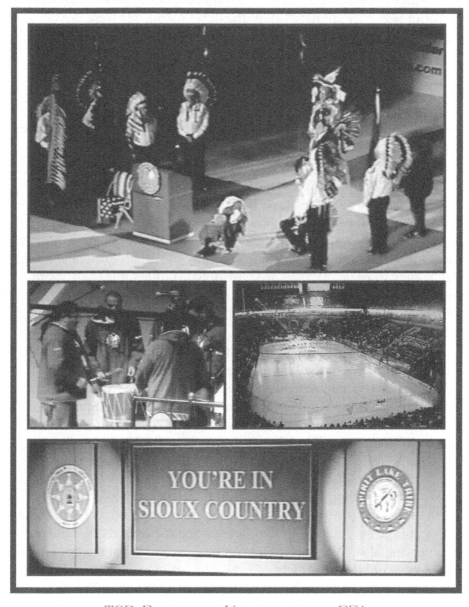

TOP: Elders and Veterans at the REA
CENTER LEFT: Drummers at the REA Flag Ceremony
CENTER RIGHT: 11,000 Fans at the REA Flag Ceremony
(Picture Courtesy of REA 10-05-2008)
BOTTOM: Standing Rock and Spirit Lake Tribal Flags at the
REA (Picture Courtesy of REA)

Protestors were aired and printed. But no one, NOT ONE, who was a supporter was ever approached by the news media nor were any statements in print from supporters.

And of the small handful of protesters, more than half were not even Native American yet they got all of the coverage. I believe most of the protesters lived in Grand Forks. Yet we supporters from Spirit Lake traveled 100 miles to attend and Standing Rock is over 300 miles away. That's one way.

I felt, surely the NCAA must see this. They started this whole mess, so they must be watching. It is pretty clear the Sioux of North Dakota support the UND Fighting Sioux name and logo, even if they're not watching, surely the university will inform them. I thought it was kind of funny though, I didn't see any university officials there. *Maybe they were out of town or something?* I didn't think any more about it. But if the NCAA was doing this out of respect for our feelings then they surely must know how we feel by now.

The holiday season was upon us and we were all busy with our families. We believed the flag raising ceremony should have accomplished the requirements needed for the NCAA. Standing Rocks Tribal flag had been hanging there for years and now the Spirit Lake flag joined it, both with support of the majority of Tribal members of the two Sioux tribes of N.D. For over 80 years, UND has carried the Sioux name. What more could the NCAA want?

We heard nothing from the NCAA, their silence was deafening. But in late 2008, it was clear, the flag ceremony was not enough. John and I got together with the committee, to explore options. We did do a little venting also. Where is all this coming from? We shared our own experiences of UND and Grand Forks. One of our committee members told us she attend the university and always felt ok there. The only place she was uncomfortable was at the Native American Center, so after a while she did not go there anymore. I shared the experience our group had at the center, when we toured UND. We were somewhat surprised, that there was no response from the UND administration. Although the new UND president, Robert Kelly had said, he and his administration were going to remain neutral on this issue and leave it to the State Board of Higher Education. We didn't find out till later that was not the case.

CHAPTER 5:
EFFORTS TO BRING ABOUT A VOTE

January 9, 2009, *(Courtesy of Kevin Fee and Grand Forks Herald): Will Summit League decision speed things up: President of the SBHE says a new timetable may be set up at the next Board meeting.

January 11, 2009, *(Courtesy of Grand Forks Herald): It's time to drop UND nickname and logo: Officials of the Summit League will not talk to UND about membership till the nickname is settled. This was something new. Although it didn't seem that important to us, it was to play a big part in the upcoming battle. (It is not the Summit league that is deceitful, but the intentional miss-use of it to justify getting rid of the name. Our opinion)

In late January 2009, we decided to work for a Tribal vote in the next election. What would it take? What would we need to do? The next Tribal election wasn't till April 21, 2009, so we had plenty of time to check on support. The NCAA deadline was almost two years away, so there is plenty of time to get this done.

Also in January although we were unaware of it, a committee was assembled at the direction of Chancellor Goetz headed by Grant Shaft, a member of the SBHE to address and find if there is support by Tribal members or not.

February 10, 2009* (Courtesy of Tu-Uyen Tran and Grand Forks Herald): Tribal Members want the nickname on the ballot: The story

53

minimizes the significance of our group by intentionally leaving out our name (Committee for Understanding and Respect). The Chancellor suggests a vote would not be enough.

Again we were unaware at the time of the one and only meeting by the SBHE committee took place on February 26th, 2009 in which Erich Longie Spirit Lake tribal member told the committee "they could only talk to Tribal Governments and not the Tribal members." Because we were unaware of just what was taking place in back rooms, everything seemed confusing to our committee and tribal members. (Courtesy of the City Beat February 26th, 2009 by TuUyen-Tran (Grant Forks Herald.)

So for January and February 2009, we talked to members as we met them. We didn't feel the need to go door to door at that time; we just talked to members as we met them. By late February, it was obvious the majority of enrolled members would like their voice heard on this issue. I talked to a Tribal council member, and asked about getting it on the spring primary ballot.

She said that although it was not needed, it would probably be helpful to have a petition done, which would force it onto the tribal agenda. So John went about drafting up the language for the petition. On March 8th, the petition was ready. We had 5 days to get enough signatures needed, due to a 30 day prior to an elections deadline, the petition needed to be in by March 13, 2009. Because we all had jobs, we could only collect names in the evening. Five evenings was not going to give us much time, but we were confident.

PETITION for REFERENDUM
THE UNDERSIGNED ENROLLED MEMBERS OF THE SPIRIT
LAKE TRIBE, IN ACCORDANCE WITH
THE PROVISIONS IN THE SPIRIT LAKE CONSTITION AND
BY LAWS, HEREBY PETITION
THE SPIRIT LAKE TRIBAL COUNCIL TO AUTHORIZE A
SPECIAL ELECTION COINCIDING WITH The 2009 PRIMARY
ELECTION TO INCLUDE A BALLOT TO DETERMINE THE
TRIBE'S APPROVAL OR DISAPPROVAL OF THE UNIVERSITY
OF NORTH DAKOTA'S ATHLETIC TEAMS TO BE KNOWN AS
THE "FIGHTING SIOUX" WITH THE RESPECTFUL LOGO

One of our committee members and I went together, as did the other committee members. We went out in 20 below zero temperatures, to get names. Out of every home we went to, only one member did not want to sign the petition and that was only because the last petition he signed, he thought it was to get rid of a pit bull dog, but it turned out to be a councilman. He had vowed never to sign another petition.

When getting the needed signatures, we never asked how they felt about the name and logo. We would tell them how we felt, only if we were asked, but we never tried to influence anyone in how to vote. I would not be surprised if some, that oppose the name and logo signed the petition as well. After we told the people signing that they should vote on the issue, however they felt about it. I felt it was that simple.

We were beginning to wonder what was really going on here. The Grand Forks Herald was printing a lot of negative stories and we were wondering just where they were all coming from, but we still thought we had an ally in the Grand Forks Herald.

March 4, 2009, *(Courtesy of Amy Dalrymple and Grand Forks Herald): "The SBHE Committee questions REA lobbying to retain nickname". *Instead of seeking and obtaining support, the committee is witch hunting (our opinion).* The story suggests that the REA is directing supporters and is falsely representing the University. It is a complete false and misleading story.

March 6, 2009, *(Courtesy of Tu-Uyen Tran and Grand Forks Herald): Nickname prompts two petitions. Erich Longie says he has a petition requesting the Tribal Council to rescind the old resolution of support from 2000. His petition goes nowhere and it is the first of many to come that go nowhere. He also repeats accusations that he believes the REA of financing supporter's effort again. He makes this accusation again and again that he thinks the REA is paying and directing the supporters on this issue. Again it is completely a false story and he knows it. The Herald finds no trouble in printing Erich's false accusations.

March 9, 2009, *(Courtesy of Amy Dalrymple and Grand Forks Herald): "Engelstads behind scholarship gift". The story suggests the Engalstad Foundation is being sneaky. The endowment is for one million dollars with first preference to the Sioux "Logical". Leigh Jeanotte Head of the Native American Center and is an enrolled member of Turtle Mountain Chippewa Tribe, in 2005 as well as other times said, there are more needy tribes than the Sioux.

We turned in our petition on March 13, 2009 with 301 signatures. Far more than the 220 signatures that was needed. Members were chasing John down the hall at the blue building Spirit Lake (TRIBAL AND BIA office building), wanting to sign as he turned in the petition. These signatures were acquired in basically 4 evenings, about 20 hours of circulating the petition. Now it was just a matter of waiting. Although we had not put on any presentations or tried to influence any one on how to vote, we were confident of the outcome.

A story is printed on March 14, 2009, *(Courtesy of Erich Longie and Grand Forks Herald): VIEWPOINT; "Common myths about logo". Erich Longie gives his opinion as if it was fact and all Sioux agreed with him. Erich states 6 myths he feels are true, but at the end he makes himself very clear, when Erich say's "don't make ME wait in line".

March 15, 2009 * (Courtesy of Grand Forks Herald), by way of Bismarck Tribune: "Change the name and logo". Tribal Leaders have said over and over again, change the name. Nothing but negative and false impression stories are making it into the press, just personal opinions. But in every story they end with the Sioux are the only ones that can save the name and logo.

April 9, 2009 *(Courtesy of Tu-Uyen Tran and Grand Forks Herald): "Sioux Tribes begin nickname campaigns"; half the story is about poor Erich and the opposition getting a late start. He states that the supporters are just getting family support. Erich is my cousin, but he had a hard time getting much of our family to agree with him. LATE START, my god, we found out later the agitators have been organized for 30 years. The same names and signatures are connected to almost every opposition letter or resolution from the 1990's and they don't seem to value the truth or have faith in tribal member's judgment. Names such as Ron His Horses Thunder, David Gipp, Leigh Jennotte, Jesse Taken Alive, Charlie Murphy, Holly Annis, Amber Annis, B.J.Rainbow, Erich Longie, Professor Lucy Gange, Professor Jim Grijalva, and organizations like American Indian Movement

56

(AIM) & Building Roads Into Diverse Groups Empowering Students (B.R.I.D.G.E.S.)

April 11, 2009 *(Courtesy of Tu-Uyen Tran and Grand Forks Herald): "The nickname, the tribes and the Ralph": a total distortion of facts. The story suggests that we are driving back and forth to Standing Rock all the time, a four hundred mile round trip (did not happen); that we are spending lots of money and the Heralds is asking, where are we getting it from (stated as if it is true, it is not)? It's suggested the Engelstad Foundation may be behind mobilizing and financing it (again not true). It questions that Sam Dupris works for the REA and what is he doing at Spirit Lake? All of what they are implying is a distortion of the truth. Almost all of it is not true, and I believe they knew it, but the truth evidently does not fit their agenda.

April 15, 2009 *(Courtesy of Eunice Davidson and Grand Forks Herald), Eunice Davidson, "Saving the nickname is enough reward" This was a letter I sent to the Herald and it was edited by the editor. He did not change it much, but it lost the message I intended to say. My message was of the distortions the Herald put out with the nickname, the tribes and the Ralph and other stories. Although it is true, saving the name would be my reward; this letter was in response to false accusations being printed over and over.

Fighting Sioux Logo

It is with regret that I feel I must write this letter to the editor. The recent article in the Grand Forks Herald and the blog of a certain Grand Forks reporter questions my honesty.

Our committee has always tried to be open and honest. When this reporter from the Grand Forks Herald called me at my home, I informed him that our committee was going to have a meeting the following week. We have always felt that it was necessary to speak as a committee and not an individual, but because I was singled out I feel it is necessary to respond.

I believe that I informed the reporter that there was a possibility that Sam Dupris was going to be at our meeting, and we see nothing wrong with that. But the meeting was not about Sam Dupris, it was about how to get the vote out, and now that it has been officially put on the ballot, we have received a few donations, and how would be the best way to use the funds.

I am a full blood, enrolled members of the Spirit Lake Tribe. For many years I have supported the "Fighting Sioux" nickname. A few years ago I called UND and informed them who I was and how I felt, and what could I do to help save the name. They informed me that I should make my feelings known, and offered to give us a tour of the UND campus. I and some of my family and friends took the tour, and while we were on campus we went to the Native American center. Their were a few students there who wanted to talk with our group. They told us their reasons they were against the name. They said they felt like they were singled out because they were Native American and were being confronted about the nickname. We listened and when they were done we asked them how is changing a name going to take away what they felt? In fact some of our group members asked if any of them were from the Dakota tribes? None of them were and we asked why they would want to change a name that has nothing to do with their heritage?

The Grand Forks Herald reporter was invited to our committee planning meeting and in our meeting we discussed certain ways of campaigning, putting out posters, radio, newspaper, & TV ads. We discussed now that we had a few donations what would be the best way to use it. Our committee has operated on our own personal income and time. This Grand Forks Herald reporter made allegations in his report, and blog that we have received funds from the "Englestad" arena. I want people to know not once has our committee ever asked for any funding, or received any. Our only request was to hang the flags from both Spirit Lake & Standing Rock Reservations in the arena. Nor have the "Englestad" people ever offered our committee or any of us anything. Yes we have gone out to lunch with Sam Dupris and he has bought a couple of us lunch, but we have also bought him lunch. It is an act of courtesy to do that,, I believe. As far as our private donations and who they come from, that is not up to our committee to release their name, if those private donors want to speak out about it that is up to them. It is only after the official notification that the vote would be on the ballot, that any pledges for donations were offered. Up until that time, everything was out of our own pockets, our committee members went out after work from house to house to get signatures on a petition to require a vote. Every one of our committee members paid for their own gas to go out and do this.

The reason I am in favor of saving the nickname "The Fighting Sioux" is just that! I am proud of the name. I have gone back into my genealogy and have found some amazing facts about my ancestors who earned the name "The Fighting Sioux", I know where it came from and who gave the Dakota that name, but I think to myself they took the derogatory name of "Sioux" and turned it into a great and powerful name. They have been called that for hundreds of years and have not whined about it. As John Chaske has said "If taking that nickname away would stop all racism or prejudice I'd do it in a second", but that is not going to do it.

I have great respect for my cousin "Erich Longie" and his opinion, but I don't happen to agree with him, we still talk and joke with each other, it's just that we have a difference of opinions.

I believe in getting this issue on the ballot lets the people decide, not just a few but the majority. I can accept if the will of the people is to drop the name, I will not be happy but I can accept that. And I would further hope that if the will of the people is to keep the name that the opposition could accept that too...

I also was totally offended by what the reporter said in his ambiguous comment that all reservation people lived in poverty - we also work for a living and earn our wages too!

There is no financial gain for me whatsoever for me or any other member, my reward would be the honor of seeing the "The Fighting Sioux" logo carried on.

Eunice Davidson
Spirit Lake Enrolled Member

April 16, 2009 *(Courtesy of Tu-Uyen Tran and Grand Forks Herald): "Fighting Sioux nickname opponents at Spirit Lake seek referendum delay: (Tribal Court case # 09-04-081 Erich Longie Terry Morgan plaintiffs v. Spirit Lake Election Board). The Herald prints the allegation by the opposition that over 85 signatures are fraudulent, again there is no evidence to support the allegation and it was later proven false. WDAZ-TV news at 10 PM carries a statement by one of the opposition leaders (tribal member) obviously upset claiming over 85 signatures are fraudulent, again with no proof. It does not state that the opposition is trying to silence the people's right through an injunction in tribal court or that the case is denied on the 17th.

April 16, 2009, The Herald neglects to mention that UND staff (Professor Amy Philips) helped the opposition in those presentations on the Spirit Lake reservation and was interviewed by the Devils Lake Journal. She also was on the WDAZ-TV 10 PM news that night, at which time an opposition leader is suggesting that there are over 85 fraudulent signatures on the petition. Nobody ever reports in fact, there were only 8 disqualified signatures and they were disqualified because one was an enrolled member of Standing Rock and six lived just off the reservation. You need to live on the reservation to qualify.

Although it got little coverage on April 17th, 2009, the court dismissed the injunction against the tribal vote and John Chaske was on WDAZ-TV expressing gratitude to the court for its ruling in favor of *Tribal members.*

April 18, 2009 *(Courtesy of Tu-Uyen Tran and Grand Forks Herald): "Nickname struggle intensifies": the story talks about the

LEFT: PROFESSOR AMY PHILIPS OF UND
(PICTURE COURTESY OF WDAZ-TV)
RIGHT: JOHN AFTER COURT DISMISSES INJUNCTION

disgusting fliers used by the opposition, although the Herald does finally states "Erich said he doesn't know where they originate, the Herald has a large story about them and more." Because opposition cannot back up the accusation of racism on campus, they have now turned to destroying a man's reputation. I won't repeat the trash they were presenting to tribal member at their presentations, but they told tribal members they had proof of where the fliers and statements came from, yet were telling the Herald they didn't know?

My husband and I attended one of the presentations put on by the opposition. We were surprised at the lack of reporting on just what those presentation focuses were on and also the lack of anything to back-up their accusation.

The stories in the Herald are filled with these charges by the opposition that was nothing more than distortions, but I guess that is what the Herald needed. I have yet to see a story about the judge dismissing the opponent's injunction against the people's rights.

April 19th, 2009, *(Courtesy of Tu-Uyen Trand and Grand Forks Herald): "Standing Rock supporters of UND nickname enter new campaign phase", Standing Rock supporters are trying to get support from all 8 district 5 of which are in South Dakota.

April 21, 2009 the big day had arrived and it turned out just as we suggested it would. 67% of Spirit Lake voters expressed support for the name and logo, and it was also a 90% eligible voter turnout (according to the 2000 Federal census). We expected support was going to be a clear victory, but because of all the misinformation that was constantly in the news, even we were pleasantly surprised with the overwhelming tally. We finally would be able to relax. The last year was pretty strenuous, but it was finally over, and we had accomplished what we thought was a positive accomplishment. What more could the NCAA need?

At this point we have 5 out of the 7 North Dakota Sioux districts on record of supporting the name and image. The districts are Cannon Ball on Standing Rock and Ft. Totten District, St. Michaels, Tokio, and Crow Hill on Spirit Lake. Only Ft. Yates and Porcupine Districts are left but have never voted. Now we have 65% of North Dakota Sioux on record of supporting the name and image what more can be needed?

But again the news coverage was mostly negative and the fight was just beginning. There was much more to come and we weren't prepared for any of it. The next few weeks would have us scratching our heads in disbelief.

CHAPTER 6: ANGER AND CONFUSION
WAS OUR VOTE FOR NOTHING?

We had been working to get the tribal members voice heard, it would be on the April 21th, 2009 ballot.

The word had spread, there was going to be a vote on Spirit Lake to possibly determine, the fate of UND Fighting Sioux name & logo. A few of the alumni sent a few donations to help get the word out to the entire reservation.

I received a call from a Grand Fork Herald reporter (Tu-Uyen Tran) asking for a statement. I informed him that we speak as a committee, not as individuals. I invited him to our next committee meeting, out of courtesy and the hopes of countering hundreds of negative stories that appear in the press. I believe it was on April 10, 2009 or so. I told him, Sam Dupris might be there, but the meeting was about the upcoming vote and not about Sam.

You see, Sam worked for the Engelstad Arena. His job was liaison between the REA and the Tribes. There was no secret there, that the REA was concerned about the outcome, as expected. MY GOD, the REA stands for Ralph Engelstad Arena and a few years before Ralph's passing, he told the University that he would build a beautiful arena for the hockey team (of which he played goalie for in his college days). He had but one stipulation, "To keep the name and logo". He built a 104 million dollar arena on that guarantee. There are over 2400

LEFT: Entrance to the Ralph Englestad Arena
RIGHT: Front of the Ralph Englestad Arena

logos throughout the REA and the cost of removing them would be tremendous, so sure the REA was concerned.

Because Sam worked for the arena, opponents found it easy with the help of the Grand Forks Herald to twist the truth through baseless and false accusation. I'm sure they knew the color of his toilet paper and the type of underwear he wore, but they could never find where he had paid anyone off, because it never happened. It must have stuck in their craw, the couple of times they did admit there was no evidence to back up the accusations. *I had asked my cousin Erich Longie once, "Why do you keep saying I and the committee are being paid when you know it's not true?" He told me not to take it personal. "It's only politics,"* But the Herald did not seem to have any trouble printing those accusations over and over without any evidence to back it up. I can only assume Erich was right "Its only politics".

The meeting did take place and Ty-Uyen did attend. Sam was also there. Sam had attended a number of our meetings. He would make suggestions. If they were helpful suggestions, we would use them; if we disagreed we would not use them. All our decisions were made as a group and everybody's ideas were heard and respected.

We had a number of meetings over the past months. Our meetings would usually be in the conference room at the Administration building or as everyone calls it the "Blue Building". They were open to anyone. At one of our first meetings, the opposition showed up. They were not there to solve any disagreements, they seemed to be there to intimidate and disrupt. Their arguments had been in the press many times, and we disagreed with them. After sometime of arguing we told them if you are here only to agitate and not to be helpful, we asked them to leave.

We know there are honorable tribal members that believe in their heart that this name and logo does not honor our history and some believe that this is an unacceptable way to honor anyone's ancestors, and they also have respect for the people and stand with them once they have spoken. They do not rely on twisting the truth or distortions or just plain distortions to accomplish their beliefs and we have respect for them. *It is the others that believe the end justifies the means* that we have problems with and they seem to be controlling the debate.

But getting back to our meeting, we discussed ways of getting our message out, we thought about fliers, TV and radio. What should the ads say? How much would they cost? Did we have enough money from donations? (It was only a couple hundred dollars.) It was decided, that we had enough money for some fliers and the tribal radio station does public service announcements free.

Again, I was amazed when I read the article by Ty-Uyen Tran in the *Grand Forks Herald on April 11th, 2009 (The nickname, the tribes and the Ralph). It is clear to us now, the media had chosen sides and the truth was not the side they choose. The story was mostly about the Engelstad Arena and Sam Dupris. There were at least 14 statements in the article that were inaccurate or misleading. I believe all 14 statements put supporter's honesty in question. By reading the article, a person would think we were putting on a multi-million dollar campaign against a poor, pitiful group. Nothing could be further from the truth!

Let me fill you in. It does not cost anything to talk to people who come to where you are. We just met people during our daily routines. That is how our surveys were done. It did take time, but it didn't cost anything. As for the petition, I paid for my gas, as did the other committee members. I spent about $25.00 on gas (At the price of gas today, I would have to take out a loan and mortgage my home haha). No one gave us a dime at that time.

As for the flag ceremony, we all paid for our own transportation. It is true that at the flag ceremony, a free lunch was served to those who came early. We also attended the hockey game free. But we were honored guests, we were there to support the continued use of our name and symbol at UND and the Engelstad arena and they in turn were honoring us as Sioux people.

For those who would say, this is bribery, let me ask you how many banquets have you attended or even heard of, that the quest of honor pays? Most are put up with a room for the night and all expenses are paid! That did not happen for us. The opposition was not at the meeting, but their baseless accusation filled the article. There was one little statement to the fact that "So far, opponents haven't produced any proof", but even that did not stop the Herald from printing them over and over and over and over and over for the past months.

Because my name was mentioned in the article, I felt I needed to respond to that article and it was printed in the "*Grand Forks Herald April 15, 2009, (Eunice Davidson; Devils Lake). I was surprised to get a call from the editor of the Herald; He said he would have to edit the article to fit, but he would get my approval before printing, which he did and I gave the okay. Because they mentioned me personally, I suppose they had to print it. To me, it seemed like any and every negative story by anyone could make it into the Grand Forks Herald, but it seemed like positive stories were few and far between and had to be edited. As committee members or individuals, our honesty and integrity was always in question and our finances were a big issue.

Eunice's Letter of April 21, 2009 as it appeared in the Herald:

Hi Tom Dennis Grand Forks Herald, would you please put this in your editorial. Please let me know what you think.

Thank You
Eunice Davidson

April 20, 2009

The Spirit Lake Committee to Save The Fighting Sioux Nickname wishes to apologize to the people of North Dakota, whether they are Native American or White. It was our wish to have an open discussion on the nickname and logo without smearing anyone's name or reputation, on either side of the issue. Furthermore, we wish to apologize to the Englestad family for the fallout they have endured from a negative campaign launched by the opposition. Without the Englestad contributions a Sioux scholarship fund would not exist at UND.

There is absolutely no defending the flyers that the opposition refers to. They are vile and disgusting, and the Native American community has every right to be angry. But the opposition does not even know where they came from. It is not out of the realm of possibilities over the years that Native Americans who oppose the name might have made such flyers to start trouble, but it is obvious that whoever they were, they did not have the guts to sign them. These racist attacks can only harm any efforts of achieving good will and understanding between UND and the Sioux people of North Dakota.

It is clear that the White community loves and honors their "Fighting Sioux" teams. They have pride in those teams and their name. They love the name and are afraid it will be taken away. They are also angry, and have a right to be. But it is also clear that this can only be decided by the Sioux Nation. It is our heritage, just as it was for the Florida Seminoles.

In spite of all this, the committee remains positive and devoted to the responsibility to protect the wellbeing of our grandchildren and future generations. We wish to leave a legacy providing educational opportunities and preserving our identity as "Fighting Sioux" for a peaceful co-existence and racial harmony through education and enlightenment. It is our desire that the people of Spirit Lake vote what their conscience compels them to.

The Spirit Lake Committee for Understanding and Respect

But no mention of the opponent's costs were ever printed or questioned. As a committee or as individuals we had addressed our expenses numerous times with reporters, but the opposition had been invited numerous times to address the students at UND. Who paid expenses? By this time, opposition leaders were putting presentation on though out Spirit Lake. Who paid for them? At those presentations, lunch was served. Who paid for that? At those presentations, a power point presentation was done and many fliers were handed out. Who paid for that? UND professor Amy Philips attended and did help with the presentation on at least one occasion. Who paid for that? Did UND help put the presentation together? If so, who paid for that? Erich Longie stated that he and others were going to homes though out the reservation and talking to members to inform them of his views, that costs money and time, why no questions about that?

On April 16, 2009, the opposition served papers to the tribal court, requesting an injunction to stop or delay the peoples voice (April 16, 2009 Petition

LEFT: LEIGH JEANOTTE FROM THE NATIVE AMERICAN CENTER
(PICTURE COURTESY OF WDAZ-TV)
RIGHT: LEIGHʼS SECRETARY AT THE CENTER, MICHELLE KNZEL

for Injunction Tribal Court case # 09-04-081). Did the UND legal department aid them in preparing the brief to the court? If so, who was paying for the time and expenses? Why no question in the herald about the opposition finances? These were some of my thoughts as this was going on?

The injunction was dismissed and the vote did take place on April 21, 2009, and as we had predicted, there was overwhelming support by the people and 67% of the voters cast their ballot in support of the name and logo to stay at UND, because we are proud of our heritage. Furthermore, we never once put on presentation or tried to influence peoples vote. Our petition only asked if they wanted a vote. Unlike opponents, who put on numerous presentations and were still unable to persuade tribal members to abandon our ancestors.

April 21st, 2009 *(Courtesy of Eunice Davidson and Grand Forks Herald): Eunice Davidson, Devils Lake, Letter: Apologies for the campaignʼs ugly turn: I was sorry and ashamed of the disgusting fliers the opposition had used to try to influence tribal member. The apology was meant for the citizens of North Dakota and the Englestad family.

The day of the vote, I called the manager at the REA to tell him what I was hearing from the Districts as the results were coming in. First was St. Michaelʼs District, which was reporting overwhelming turn out and it was all positive for us supporters.

April 22, 2009 Courtesy of WDAZ-TV news story: *Leigh Jeanotte head of the Native American Center at UND and a mixed blood Chippewa in response to the vote "if they were more educated, they would have made a better decision" also that" level headed individuals would agree with him"*, I thought to myself when I heard this on the news, what kind of person who works in the education field comes out and tell us the Sioux that we are stupid? Scary!

April 23rd, 2009 *(Courtesy of Jim Grijalva and Grand Forks Herald), column, *Professor Jim Grijalva at the UND school of law: "A third issue is whether the new discussion has intellectual integrity or simply is result-oriented hypocrisy".* I thought who is this guy and a lawyer at that, to question a tribe's right to vote and the democratic system. I hate to use the word "racist" but that is what came to my mind.

Both judgmental statements question the intellectual ability of the Sioux people of Spirit Lake and no one in the media thought anything about them or do they agree with them? Is it not considered to being Biased, Bigoted, Racist or Elitist to question the intelligence of a people, simply because they disagree with you?

But the vote had taken place, even with all the obstacles placed in front of it, and it confirmed what we had been saying for months, the proof was now there for all to see, it cannot be denied or so we thought.

Within a week after the vote, rumors were flying. The North Dakota State Board of Higher Education was going to retire the name and logo at their next meeting on May 14, 2009. We were beginning to wonder "what the hell is going on here?" What do we have to do? We hoped the rumors were not true, but for the first time we asked for help. We contacted Jody Hodgson at the REA. We informed him of how the State Board of Higher Education, although they agreed in the settlement to seek support from the tribes, *was as it seemed to us,* avoiding and denying a voice to supporters. We wanted an opportunity to share our views, but to this point nobody seemed interested.

Jody got back to us; I believe it was on May 8, 2009. He said a meeting was set up for May 10, 2009 at the North Dakota Attorney General's office, if we could make it. I don't know who put the pressure on, but we were finally going to be able to speak to a State Board official in person. It was short notice, but after months of *rejection* we had a meeting finally.

My husband and I drove to Bismarck the night before the meeting as did John Chaske. We stayed at the Kelly Inn (Which we paid for ourselves and our gas and food as well.) and that evening we drove to Standing Rock to meet with Archie Fool Bear and Tom Iron to talk about tomorrow's meeting. They told us of the battles they were having on Standing Rock just to be allowed to talk about the issue.

In the morning we met for breakfast with Archie Fool Bear, Tom Iron, Sam Dupris and John Chaske. I had spoken to Archie on the phone, but I had never met him till last night. I had met Tom once and that was on April 11, 2009 at one of our committee meetings.

After breakfast, we all met at the state capital building and went to the Attorney General's office. We had to wait in the secretary's office for about 20 minutes and it was the most enjoyable time of the whole trip. The guys started teasing David about his hair and how he looked like "Fonzy" from Happy Days the way he was standing. It progressed from Brylcreem to Vaseline and on to Axel grease to control hair. By the time we were called into the AG's office, Tom insisted as a joke, that Dave go first, "He's our interpreter". Ha...

Now you need to know that from early 2007 till now May 10, 2009, I and we as a committee had been working on our own. We had met Jody Hodgson once at the flag ceremony, but that was it. Everything we had done was out of respect and pride for our people and ancestors and our passion for the Fighting Sioux name and logo.

But here we were heading into the State Attorney General's office to meet with the State Board Chancellor, as we walked into his office, Attorney General Wayne Stenehjem said that he supports the name and logo, but for this meeting he is neutral, just kind of a referee. At the meeting was, the Attorney General, Chancellor Goetz and his attorney Pat Seaworth, Sam Dupris from Cheyenne River S.D., Archie Fool Bear and Tom Iron from Standing Rock, John Chaske and myself from Spirit Lake and my husband Dave.

After introductions we sat down. Sam spoke first. Spirit Lake just spoke loud and clear; just 3 weeks ago 67% support the name and logo. Why are you going to retire the name and logo almost 2 years ahead of the deadline? No real answer was provided.

Then Archie spoke, he said the majority of enrolled members of Standing Rock support the name and logo and Cannon Ball is on record, but more importantly, a Sacred Ceremony was performed in 1969 which can never be undone, as a Sovereign Nation, to reject our sacred ceremonies and traditions would be the same as rejecting us. Again there was no response from Chancellor Goetz or his attorney.

John talked about the obstacles that we faced on Spirit Lake and yet 67% came out in support of the name and logo. What is the rush?

I talked about how honored our members and I felt about the name and logo. All questions were met with silence.

Then my husband asked the Chancellor; "Why" haven't you met with supporters from the two reservations? It is clear who they are. No response was given and then he told the Chancellor, "If you cut short the deadline, you know that the Sioux will be blamed! God knows, we don't want it to happen, but realistically we know someone is probably going to get physically hurt from your decision and you will be too blame". Again, there was no real response. Then he asked point blank "HAVE YOU MET WITH THE OPPOSITION?"; to which the Chancellor turned to his attorney who said "Not officially".

To all of us, we felt like the Chancellor was looking down his nose at us, because his head was tilted back and his nose was so high in the air. It may be just the way he is, but none of us got a good feeling from him.

From our perspective, nothing had been accomplished at the meeting. We believed they had no interest in us or our people as well as the name and image, they had the opportunity to communicate their position on the issue at that time, but chose to be silent. As we got outside the Capital building, we shook hands with Archie, Tom and Sam. We looked at each other, in disappointment and said "Well we tried", and then drove home.

As my husband and I drove home, it was clear my husband was more than disappointed. I was discouraged to say the least, but my husband was visibly mad. He said the words I heard him say so many times "Another black eye I have to carry because of those sneaky, slimy White Bastards", referring to white politicians dealing with Native Americans.

When we got home and for the next couple of days, we were feeling kind of down. But on May 12, 2009 I got a call from Earl Strinden a representative from the Ralph Englestad Arena, he said, "I don't know what you folks said, but the State Board has agreed to put you on the agenda if you can make it to Dickenson on May 14th, 2009.

Again, this was short notice and most committee members were going to be unable to make it. John and I were going to be there come hell or high water. By this time I and my husband were working for a museum in Devils Lake and I talked to the Board of Directors. They had no problem with us missing work as long as someone could cover for us.

For those who are wondering "What is this white man (Dave Davidson) doing in there?" First, what affects me also affects my husband. Second, yes, my husband is a full blood Norwegian, but since the age of 7, his life has been more connected to Native American's then non-Natives. From his early years when his closest friends were a mixed blood Chippewa family, at the age of 11 spending summers at the Jetty home where his sister was married to my future foster brother, to quitting school at 15 and moving to the Jetty farm year round, to being a Foreman for a local construction company for 18 years that employed many Spirit Lake members, to working for the tribal chemical abuse program, to getting his GED with help from the Spirit Lakes Little Hoop community college, to helping me and other tribal members with family trees (including my cousin Erich), to researching treaties with the Dakota and U S government starting in 1815. He brings a unique perspective to the table; because of his caring for my people I offered tobacco to my Uncle to give Dave an Indian name, and he was given one in a ceremony in a sweat lodge. His given Dakota name is "MatoMani' (Walking Bear). My hubby has expressed many times how honored he was to receive such a gift.

Chapter 7:
The Next Step Another Ambush

But back to the topic at hand, we arrived in Dickenson about 7:00 PM on the 13th of May. We checked into a room and then looked for Sam and John. We found Sam but John hadn't arrived yet. John did arrive shortly after we found Sam. After John checked in, the four of us sat down in the lobby and talked about what we expected tomorrow at the meeting. Sam also gave us a copy of the court Settlement/Agreement. This was the first time we actually saw the full court agreement.

After talking for a while we all went our separate ways for the evening. Dave and I went to Perkins for supper and as usual we ordered something that also gave pancakes. Dave is nuts about the syrups.

While there we read through the Settlement/Agreement. After supper we went back to our room and read the settlement again. We also called Archie, to see if he was coming. He said it was just too short of a notice and he was unable to attend.

The morning of the State Board meeting we were up early and met in the lobby again. We went over last minute strategies before heading off to the meeting. We got to Dickenson State University around 8:15 AM. A lady asked if we were the group of supporters. We informed her we were. She asked us to take a seat in the hallway and that she would be right back.

GRANT SHAFT ND STATE BOARD MEMBER AND HEAD OF THE
COMMITTEE ON THE FIGHTING SIOUX ISSUE.
(COURTESY OF WDAZ-TV)

She returned a couple of minutes later with Grant Shaft, who is a
member of the State Board of Higher Education and appointed by
Chancellor Goetz to oversee this issue. We all introduced ourselves
and then Grant Shaft knelt down in front of us. He said the agenda was
very strict, so there would be limited time for our presentation. He said
we would be given 5 minutes each. My husband then asked if he could
say a few words, but was told no "because the agenda time was so
limited, there would be no time for it", if you weren't on the agenda
you would have to wait until the meeting adjourns to give input. My
husband said he understood, but we now feel as though behind his nice
smile was a hand with a knife.

At 8:45 AM on May 14, 2009, the meeting was called to order.
The normal business was attended to first as things usually go, and
then about 10:00 AM, Grant Shaft was asked to give his report on the
name and logo issue.

The mad scramble that took place was hilarious. Reporters were falling all over themselves to get their video cameras and tape recorders set up. One camera man tripped on the table in front of us and almost fell completely to the floor with his camera. It was clear to everyone, this was the issue everyone was interested in, especially the media.

Mr. Shaft took the floor. He reported that scheduled committee meetings with the tribal leadership had been unsuccessful. So there was no movement in that area. He talked about the Summit League and the need to hurry, (which is crap, as you will find out later) and 15 minutes before the morning break at 10:15 AM, we supporters were called up.

Sam spoke first, in his presentation he spoke about the fact that just over three weeks ago Spirit Lake voted 67% in support of the name and logo. He spoke about the very strong evidence that Standing Rock would do the same if and when they get to vote. He spoke to the fact that even if accepted by the Summit League which was not guaranteed UND would not have any games until at least the fall of 2011. Why is there such a rush now? The deadline isn't until Nov. 30, 2010.

John spoke next. He talked about how he is now one of the elders of the tribe and is also a spiritual leader. He spoke to the significance of the SACRED CEREMONY performed in 1969 and how once the SACRED PIPE has been smoked, it can never be undone. As traditional people, that ceremony cannot be dismissed without dismissing us as a people.

I was up next and spoke about how our people and how much pride they feel in the name and logo. I was unaware that Ron His Horses Thunder (Standing Rocks Tribal Chairman) had just walked into the room a few minutes earlier and I was interrupted in my presentation by Duane Espegard of the State Board.

He said, *"I see the Tribal Chairman from Standing Rock is here, we would like to hear a few words from him"* and he asked Ron His Horses Thunder to come up and take the microphone. Which he did, cutting short our one and only time to address the full board. There was about 3 minutes to go before the morning break when the Chairman began to speak. Remember the agenda MUST BE

74

STRICKLY FOLLOWED, but evidently it no longer applied, because His Horses Thunder proceeded to *"spew, what I consider garbage"* for about 20 minutes. Well beyond the **"Strict Agenda"** time limit, and he was not on the agenda, like we were.

The Standing Rock Chairman came up and stood right behind Sam, John and I. He started off with anyone who supports the name and logo, is promoting racism. Then proceeded to run down almost every white person (including the more than 60 in the room) and I am still trying to figure out what Aunt Jemima has to do with it, but toward the end he finally said something relevant. He said (as he tapped Sam on the shoulder and told him to take notes), *"I don't care if 100% of the people of Standing Rock sign a petition in support of the name and logo, I will roll it up and throw it in the garbage. "I have that power" and furthermore that ceremony from 1969, means nothing! "The man is dead" and with a hand motion he said "puff it's gone"!!*

I almost fell out of my chair, and this man claims to be trying to preserve our culture, traditions, and heritage and is supposedly a distant descendant of Sitting Bull, but this evidently is what he truly believes of our culture and traditions.

About half way through his presentation, I couldn't take it anymore and got up and went and sat next to my husband, in the audience. My husband was so angry, that he tried to say something after His Horses Thunder was done, but they cut the microphone and ordered him to sit down or leave. There were about 60 people in the room that heard it, but the meeting was adjourned for morning break.

As we left the conference room, there stood Ron His Horses Thunder and Duane Espegard, with Duane's arm around Ron's shoulder and shaking hands. There was a big smile on their faces, like the cat that ate the canary (my opinion of course).

I feel it must be pointed out that the trip from Standing Rock to Dickenson is about two hours. The Chairman came in just a little over two hours late and it was just a little over two hours from the time the Board knew we were there to testify and also he was not on the strict agenda, **just food for thought.**

We were standing about 25 feet away in the hallway when Duane Espergard came stomping over to just inches in front of Sam, with anger in his eye, he commenced to tell Sam, *" I took offence to your questions, who are you to question us"? Sam tried to apologize, stating that he didn't mean to offend anyone, but Duane said again "NO, I will not accept your apology with his finger almost in Sam's face. "I WILL NEVER ACCEPT YOUR APPOLIGY"* and turned and stomped away.

In somewhat of a shock, we went and sat down in the hallway. Grant Shaft came over to us and said *"Don't let Ron upset you, the board has a standing joke, here comes Ron hide the mic."* He continued to say that they have heard it all hundreds of times before. Which leads to the question "WHY" was he needed to speak again, the same words the Board heard hundreds of times?

We felt like we had been set-up by the Board calling on His Horses Thunder to counter us and we couldn't wait to get the hell out of there. We went to Applebee's and had lunch before heading home. We shared our thoughts about the morning. We all felt like, we had been ambushed again. We were completely stunned by Ron's statement towards the members of Standing Rock and of our Sacred Ceremony.

On our way home, less than 20 miles out of Dickenson they announced that the State Board had just retired the name and logo. It did not surprise us though, by now it was starting to become clearer, at least to us, the State Board had decided long ago to retire the name and logo. It seemed evident, they did not want to be held responsible for it and we were thinking, just what was the 2007 Settlement/Agreement all about?

That became even clearer when the newspapers reported the story. What was decided by the State board "Standing Rock was given till Sept, 2009 to give support and Spirit Lake as well as Standing Rock had to give a thirty year guarantee. In my mind, that was put in place just to make it more difficult to fulfill requirements in the settlement agreement. It was first suggested the date be Aug 1, 2009 by Grant Shaft, "May 14th' 2009 SBHE minutes".

They knew the current chairman of Standing Rock would be in office until at least the end of Sept, 2009. This does in fact, all but

76

guarantee that the terms of the new requirement from the State Board could not be completed. It is also in violation of the original Settlement. (State Board minutes May 14th, 2009 on page 3).

Although the original Settlement/Agreement requires any modifications to be done in writing beforehand and that both parties must agree, in this case the Executive Committee was aware of the movement on Standing Rock and Spirit Lake's vote and must have wanted an early retirement also and is silent on this violation. (See settlement/agreement)

The 18 month early deadline date as well as the "30" year guarantee clearly, drastically changes the complete Settlement/Agreement, but it also fits the NCAA's Executive Committee's desire.

Chapter 8:

THINGS ARE BECOMING CLEAR

As my husband and I drove home from Dickenson, we talked over the events of the last couple of years. I just could not understand what was going on. We believed the North Dakota Attorney General took the NCAA to court to keep the name and logo in 2006. If they didn't want to keep it, why would they have gone to court? I was sure it cost a lot of money. Money if they weren't trying to save the name and image would not have had to be wasted. So we foolishly thought there must be support in the State Board and UND, otherwise they are wasting time, money, and working everybody up for nothing.

We now have read the "settlement/agreement and mutual release" page 3 section a – University of North Dakota will be provided a period of time until November 30, 2010 (the "Approval Period") to seek and obtain namesake approval for its nickname and related imagery, from both the Spirit Lake Tribe and the Standing Rock Tribe. At this point we hadn't seen the original lawsuit and were unaware of the direction it was supposed to have been followed.

But something that caught my husband's eye, that I never saw any significance in, was on page 4 section c of the Settlement/Agreement, " by any individual duly authorized to bind or speak on behalf of Spirit Lake" whereas for Standing Rock " adopt by any means allowed in the Tribe's Constitution". I thought it was no big deal. He was puzzled as to why it wouldn't read the same for both tribes. Here again, things are clear when you know the whole story.

Unknown to us at the time: with the modification adopted by the Standing Rock Council in May of 2008, barring any discussion on the name and image issue along with the Spirit Lake Chairwoman's statement that she personally opposes the name and image, the Executive Committee, North Dakota State Board of Higher Education, University of North Dakota Administration and Attorney General were all secure with a guarantee of retirement. They didn't count on the resolve of Tribal members.

My husband, who to this point had only attended a couple of committee meetings asked, "has the State Board ever contacted any of your committee members?" I told him "no" not that I know of. He was quite puzzled. It is absolutely clear who you guys are. With all the false accusation made against you guys, it seems strange that the State Board wouldn't at least try to get your side of the story. In the agreement, it is a requirement?

I called Archie as we drove home, to fill him in on the day's proceedings. He was in shock and I don't know if he truly believed me, when I told him of what His Horses Thunder said. He hadn't heard yet, that the board had retired the name and logo, but he was disappointed to say the least when I told him, but waged to continue to fight on for his people's rights.

It is a four and a half hour drive from Dickenson to Devils Lake, so it was quite late before we got home and we were tired. So we didn't pay attention to the news that night, but the next day again we were amazed at the news coverage "again"!!

My husband, who is very suspicious of officials and their motives, had been recording the news reports on the WDAZ-TV station since the day Professor Amy Philips was on Spirit Lake (April 16, 2009) trying to influence Spirit Lake voters to oppose the name and logo, and nothing was adding up for him.

As we listened to the radio the news was State Board votes unanimous to retire name and logo, but if Standing Rock shows support by September 15, 2009, the board would revisit the issue.

To revisit the issue, now that sounds like they are respectful and trying to do the right thing. But you must know a few things, first:

79

Standing Rocks Chairman, His Horses Thunder, said the people of Standing Rock, will never have a vote, as long as he is in Chairman. And even if he's not, it will be hard for a new Chairman to allow a vote after taking office (because of certain accomplishments under His Horse's administration). Second: A new requirement was added by the State Board, "a 30 year guarantee". A new requirement that we later found out was, a forfeiture of a right that the State Board itself was barred from doing. Yet they were demanding from two Sovereign Nations to do so. Also in the Settlement/Agreement on page 9, line 5 states clearly "Any modifications to the Agreement must be in writing and executed by UND and the NCAA,_which was never done and should have voided the Settlement/Agreement".

The revised deadline date went from Aug. 1 to Sept. 15 to Oct.1 to Oct. 15 of 2009. The Standing Rock Primary was in July, they knew the Chairman was not going to allow it to be on the ballot at that time. So the date went to Oct. 1st.

They said they thought the general election was Sept.15th, but I don't know if I believe them, but it wasn't held until Sept. 30th and they then moved the deadline date to Oct 15th. That only gave, should there be a new Chairman, 15 days to have the election certified and get sworn in, have a special election to fill his old seat and forfeit Sovereignty rights. It is QUITE A DEAL.

The decision by the State Board to retire the Name and Logo 18 months ahead of the Settlement/Agreement prompted a young lady on our reservation to state what most of us felt: *"why did they have us vote if we mean nothing?"* as she was interviewed by WDAZ TV news.

Our committee still wanted to believe we were working with honorable people, toward a common goal and we continued to trust. My husband on the other hand, was getting more and more suspicious of the whole bunch. Go ahead and call us "fools" but we had never worked with such devious and sneaky people before. This was all new to us. The committee decided, we would try to help Archie on Standing Rock. We had to be careful, because we did not want in any way to be interfering in the sovereignty of Standing Rock. We were the Committee for Understanding and Respect and just as we expected

Standing Rock to respect Spirit Lake's sovereignty, we would respect there's.

That does not mean we can't have contact, it means that we will not try to control them in any way, but when advice or opinions are asked for, we well give them. We would share any knowledge we might have with Archie and his group and it is up to them as to how or if they wanted to use it.

Archie did ask for how our petition was "worded" and I e-mailed him a copy. I also sent him copies of our letters to the editors. Archie told us of how the opposition was dumping those same fliers all around the reservation and presenting them as facts. The only provable fact about them is that they do exist. Where they come from is very much in doubt.

Even Erich Longie, who at his presentation on Spirit Lake, said he could prove where they came from, but to the press admitted he did not know. It seems as though the same tactics were being used on Standing Rock. The clear fact is, no one truly knows where they came from, and they even could have come from the UND's Native American Center, where Leigh Jeanotte, who has said he's been fighting for over 30 years to get rid of the name and logo, is in charge of the Native Center at UND. (my opinion)

Is there racism, sadly the answer is yes, and it exists in every community, not just the "white community". But as John has said many times and we all agree with "if changing the name and logo would end racism, we would do it in a heartbeat" but it will not and the fact is that if you make someone give up something they love, because you personally don't like it, you will create hatred and racism. No one has proven even one case where a person became a racist because of hearing a name or seeing a logo.

But getting back to the news coverage, one cannot help but wonder, was I at the same meeting?

(Courtesy of Chuck Haga and Grand Forks Herald) May 14, 2009: "It's time for the university to move on." The story is almost all about Summit League (what a bunch of crap!) with its benefits and almost nothing about Spirit Lake or Standing Rock. President Kelley believes the North Dakota State Board of Higher Education actions seal the fate of the Fighting Sioux name.

Minutes from state board education meeting May 14, 2009. We acquired a copy a few months later -"Spirit Lake asks not to shorten timeline" and "Ron His Horse is Thunder provides testimony on voting process on Standing Rock". (Page 3)

"Are you kidding me"? The coverage by the press and State board minutes is nothing but a white wash of what actually took place (my opinion). The way the reporters acted and tripped all over themselves, when the subject came to the floor, I would have expected headlines like this, "Chairman vows never to let members of Standing Rock have a voice and sacred Indian ceremonies mean nothing"!! As to the Minutes of the State Board of Higher Education, nothing was written in the minutes about the actual testimony.

Was this story not news worthy? Did the members of Standing Rock not have a right to know what their leader said about them and their ceremonies? Did the people of North Dakota not have a right to know that "one man was determining the fate of their beloved University name"? Was this not one of the biggest stories in the state in years? Was the Chairman using the State Board to get what he wanted or was the State board using him, to get justification for what they wanted? I don't know, but I was starting to wonder if my husband might be right?

Think about this, the Norwegians have Norway to go back to for traditions and customs, the French have France, the English have England, etc. and for us Native Americans, we have our tribes to carry on our traditions and customs. What was said at the board meeting was that tribal people have no voice, they are nothing and our Sacred Ceremonies mean nothing. That the tribal officials are the only voices that count. This is something you would expect from the former Soviet Union, but here in the United States, it goes against everything we stand for. Sadly, a precedent has been established now "Tribal members mean nothing to the State Board of Higher Education or the Establishment".

If you think this is meaningless, look at our judicial system today. Court Rulings today are not made on law, but on precedence. Past case rulings justify court decisions, not the letter of law. That Also Will Show Up Later.

As Native Americans our customs, "Traditions" and "Sacred Ceremonies" define who we are. To allow individual tribal leaders total control to enforce their own personal views against the will of the people is deadly. Precedence has been set. The people's voice means nothing and our traditions mean nothing. As a people, we are becoming irrelevant. The State Board did not question him on the rationale of his decision, but seemed to encourage it. Did it fit their current agenda now? Did they need the Chairman for cover?

But here we are, it has come down to this point that the fate of the Fighting Sioux stands in the hands of Standing Rock and its Chairman, two thirds of which is in South Dakota. Even there it appears the majority support the name and logo. If not for the Standing Rock Chairman and 8 of 17 voting council members, who have worked to silence the people, the NCAA's new Settlement requirements would be more than fulfilled.

Our only avenue now was to assist Archie and his group as they fought for their people's rights. Now this has become a fight, not just for the rights of Standing Rock, it was turning into the rights of all Native people to keep their Sacred Ceremonies, their traditions, their beliefs and their identities. There are over 500 recognized tribes in the U.S. and everyone has their own tribal identity. We are not just Indians without faces, we have meaning and purpose.

In researching my family tree, we found out many things that have been and are continuing to be left out of the history books or distorted to make a completely different impression than the actual truth. My ancestors were not wimps that cried about somebody hurting their feelings, don't do that please, oh please take care of me. My ancestors were Dakota and Cut Head Sioux and darn proud of it! They just did what needed to be done, instead of whining about it.

Getting back to the summer and fall of 2009, we were in contact with Archie as spokesman for the group on Standing Rock. They were trying desperately to have the tribal members voices heard and were running into stone walls everywhere they turned.

June 4th, 2008 *(Courtesy of Joseph Marks and Grand Forks Herald): "Tribal council bans vote on nickname", the Standing Rock Council placed a moratorium early in May on any reservation wide referendum to gauge tribal support for UND's nickname.

In May of 2008, the Standing Rock Council under His Horses Thunder had managed to modify the Tribal Constitution and put a moratorium on any discussion of the Name and Logo. The vote was 7 to 5 with two members abstaining and two of the Council members absent. The motion was made by Jesse Taken Alive from the Wakpala District in South Dakota where the High School sports team is called the Fighting Sioux.

In June of 2008 Chairman Ron His Horses Thunder and the Council tried to change the name of the tribe from Standing Rock Sioux to Standing Rock Oyate, as the Sisseton/Wahpeton Tribe had done 6 years earlier. But Standing Rock tribal members shot it down, they also have pride in just who they are. In Sioux, the word Oyate means *"people"* and for some time now those opposed to the name and image have accused the Chippewa of putting the name Sioux on us. Supposedly it means "snake in the grass", but in truth it comes from the Nadouessioux an Algonquin word meaning "with whom we fight".

What Archie and his group were trying to fight was a moratorium that under his and other opinions was illegally adopted. If left it would require three quarters of the Council to vote to remove it. They were getting legal opinions and trying the courts, tribal and district, to no avail. Our dear friend Tom Irons gave us a copy of former Tribal Attorney's letter stating his legal opinion on the SR moratorium.

But as the summer rolled on, it became clear that Standing Rock members were probably going to be denied their voice. The Tribal Council controlled Tribal Court and the North Dakota District Court was refusing to get involved in tribal matters, other options needed to be explored.

STANDING ROCK SIOUX TRIBE
LEGAL DEPARTMENT
LETTER OPINION
2009-BAK-3

December 7, 2009

Mr. Tom Iron
P.O. Box 142
McLaughlin, South Dakota 57642

Dear Mr. Iron:

Thank you for your question regarding the legality of a Tribal Council motion/resolution calling for a moratorium on a referendum vote. Based on the following, it is my opinion that a motion/resolution placing a moratorium on a referendum/initiative vote is in violation of Article XI § 1 & 8 of the Constitution of the Standing Rock Sioux Tribe as well as §1302 of the Indian Civil Rights Act of 1968 (25 U.S.C. §§ 1301-03).

PROCEDURAL HISTORY

At the May 8, 2008 Tribal Council meeting a motion (#33) was made by Jesse Taken Alive, seconded by Avis Little eagle, to approve to establish a moratorium on the referendum vote to the U.N.D. logo issue, by resolution (No. 208-08). This motion passed with 7 YES votes, 5 NO votes, 1 NOT voting, and 4 excused.

At the August 11, 2009 Tribal Council meeting a motion (#22) was made by Joe White Mountain, seconded by Robert Cordova, to rescind resolution No. 208-08, passed by the Tribal Council on May 8, 2008 that put a moratorium on the U.N.D. logo. This motion failed with 7 YES votes, 8 NO votes, 1 NOT voting, and 1 excused.

ANALYSIS

Article III § 1 of the North Dakota Constitution states that the people reserve the power to propose and enact laws by the initiative… to approve or reject legislative Acts. Article III § 1 of the South Dakota Constitution states that the people expressly reserve to themselves the right to propose measures… and also the right to require that any laws which the Legislature may have enacted shall be submitted to a vote of the electors of the state before going into effect.

Article XI § 1 of the Constitution of the Standing Rock Sioux Tribal Article and §1302 of the Indian Civil Rights Act of 1968 (25 U.S.C. §§ 1301-03) both state that no Indian tribe in exercising powers of self-government shall make or enforce any law prohibiting the free exercise of religion, or abridging the freedom of speech, or of the press, or the right of the people

peaceably to assemble and to petition for a redress of grievances. Additionally, Article XI § 8 of the Constitution of the Standing Rock Sioux Tribe states that the Tribe shall not deny any person within its jurisdiction the equal protection of its laws or deprive any person of liberty or property without due process of law.

A referendum is defined as; 1) the principle or practice of referring measures proposed or passed by a legislative body to the vote of the electorate for approval or rejection; 2) A direct vote on an issue of public policy, such as a proposed amendment to a state constitution or a proposed law. Referendums, which allow the general population to participate in policy making, are not used at the national level, but are common at the state and local levels. A referendum is often used to gauge popular approval or rejection of laws recently passed or under consideration by a state legislature. A referendum can also be used to initiate legislation. http://dictionary.reference.com/browse/referendum, December 7, 2009. An initiative is defined as a procedure enabling a specified number of voters by petition to propose a law and secure its submission to the electorate or to the legislature for approval. http://dictionary.reference.com/browse/initiative, December 7, 2009. Liberty is defined as freedom from arbitrary or despotic government or control. http://dictionary.reference.com/browse/liberty, December 7, 2009.

When decisions are made by the Tribal Council, whether it is the adoption of a code or ordinance or the prohibition of certain acts by the people, individuals who may disagree are afforded the right to redress or grieve that issue through the process of referendum or initiative. Taking away that right vests more power in the Tribal Council than the Constitution of the Standing Rock Sioux Tribe permits. Tribal Council actions that limit the peoples' rights are despotic in nature and violate the peoples' right to liberty.

CONCLUSION

The passage of a motion/resolution by Tribal Council placing a moratorium on a referendum/initiative vote regarding any issue negates the peoples' right to redress their grievances regarding that issue. This is a direct violation of Article XI § 1 of the Constitution of the Standing Rock Sioux Tribe as well as §1302 of the Indian Civil Rights Act of 1968 (25 U.S.C. §§ 1301-03). Additionally, it denies the peoples' right to liberty without the due process of law violating Article XI § 8 of the Constitution of the Standing Rock Sioux Tribe.

Sincerely,

Brent A. Kary, Tribal Attorney
Standing Rock Sioux Tribe

Cc: Charles W. Murphy, Chairman
        File

LETTER FROM FORMER STANDING ROCK TRIBAL ATTORNEY
BRENT CAREY
(TEXT AS FOLLOWS)

December 7, 2009

Mr. Tom Iron
P.O. Box 142
McLaughlin, South Dakota 57642

Dear Mr. Iron:
Thank you for your question regarding the legality of a Tribal Council motion/resolution calling for a moratorium on a referendum vote. Based on the following, it is my opinion that a motion/resolution placing a moratorium on a referendum/initiative vote is in violation of Article XI § 1 & 8 of the Constitution of Standing Rock Sioux Tribe as well as § 1302 of the Indian Civil Rights Act of 1968 (25 U.S.C. §§ 1301-03).

Procedural History

At the May 8, 2008 Tribal Council meeting a motion (#33) was made by Jesse Taken Alive, seconded by Avis Little Eagle, to approve to establish a moratorium on the referendum vote to the U.N.D. logo issue, by resolution (No. 208-08). This motion passed with 7 yes votes, 5 no vote, 1 not voting, and 4 excused.

At the August 11, 2009 Tribal Council meeting a motion (#22) was made by Joe White Mountain, seconded by Robert Cordova, to rescind resolution No. 208-08, passed by the Tribal Council on May 8, 2008 that put a moratorium on the U.N.D. logo. This motion failed with 7 yes votes, 8 no votes, 1 not voting, and 1 excused.

Analysis

Article III § 1 of the North Dakota Constitution states that the people reserve the power to propose and enact laws by the initiative... to approve or reject legislative Acts. Article III § 1 of the South Dakota Constitution states that the power expressly reserved to themselves the right to propose measures... and also the right to require that any law which the Legislature may have enacted shall be submitted to a vote of the electors of the state before going into effect.

Article XI § 1 of the Constitution of the Standing Rock Sioux Tribal Constitution and § 1302 of the Indian Civil Rights Act of 1968 (25 U.S.C. §§ 1301-03) both state that no Indian tribe in exercising powers of self-government shall make or enforce any law prohibiting the free exercise of religion, or abridging the freedom of speech, or of the press, or the right of the people peaceably to assemble and to petition for a redress of grievances. Additionally, Article XI § 8 of the Constitution of the Standing Rock Tribe states that the Tribe shall not deny any person within its jurisdiction the equal protection of its laws or deprive any person of liberty or property without due process of law.

A referendum is defined as: 1) the principle or practice of referring measures proposed or passed by a Legislative body to the vote of the electorate for approval or rejection; 2) A direct vote on an issue of public policy, such as a proposed amendment to a state constitution or a proposed law. Referendums, which allow the general population to participate in policy making, are not used at the national level, but are common at the state and local levels. A referendum is often used to gauge popular approval or rejection of laws recently passed or under consideration by a state Legislature. A referendum can also be used to initiate Legislation.

http://reference.com/browse/referendum, December 7, 2009. An initiative is defined as a procedure enabling a specified number of voters by petition to propose a law and secure its submission to the electorate or to the Legislature for approval.

http://dictionary, reference.com/browse/initiative, December7, 2009. Liberty is defined as freedom from arbitrary or despotic government or control.

http://dictionary,reference.com/browse/liberty. December 7, 2009.

When decisions are made by the Tribal Council, whether it is the adoption of a code or ordinance or the prohibition of certain acts by the people, individuals who may disagree are afforded the right to redress or grieve that issue through the process of referendum or initiative. Taking away that right vests more power in the Tribal Council than the Constitution of the Standing Rock Sioux Tribe permits. Tribal Council actions that limit the peoples' rights are despotic in nature and violate the peoples' right to liberty.

Conclusion

The passage of a motion/resolution by Tribal Council placing a moratorium on a referendum/initiative vote regarding any issue negates the peoples' right to redress their grievances regarding that issue. This is a direct violation of Article XI § I of the Constitution of the standing Rock Sioux Tribe as well as § 1302 of the Indian Civil Rights Act of 1968 (25 U.S.C. §§ 1301-03). Additionally, it denies the peoples' right to liberty without the due process of law violating Article XI § 8 of the Constitution of the Standing Rock Tribe.

Sincerely,

Brent A. Kary

Tribal Attorney
Standing Rock Sioux Tribe

CC: Charles W. Murphy, Chairman File

CHAPTER 9: CONTINUING THE FIGHT

Things were looking dim, but we would not give up. It is becoming an issue of the rights of the people of Standing Rock (of which we can only give vocal support) and respect for the people of Spirit Lake. Archie has vowed to fight for his people and we can only assist him though advice and research.

As the campaign for tribal chairman waged on at Standing Rock in the summer of 2009, Charlie Murphy (a candidate for chairman) vowed he would work to allow the people a voice on this issue if elected. We were encouraged by his statements, but we had seen too much, to just sit back now. We would be limited on what we could do, without interfering with sovereignty rights.

Our main direction would be to work for the original deadline to be followed. It was going to be very difficult, due to the apparent lack of interest in keeping the Name and Logo, by the State Board of Higher Education and the media.

Throughout the summer, every week or so there would be a statement from some board member on TV or in the newspaper, as to the current status of the name and logo. Along with demand for a "30" year agreement, were the comments of, no movement on Standing Rock. Need for a resolution because of the Summit League (I won't even tell you what I was thinking at this time).

The primary was held on Standing Rock, July 15th 2009. The top 3 finishers were, Charlie Murphy (565 votes) followed by Ron His Horses Thunder (220 votes) and Avis Little Eagle (219 votes) as reported on July 20th, 2009. Of the three, only Charlie Murphy had expressed support for the name and logo. Charlie also had said he would work to allow tribal members a voice.

As for us back at Spirit Lake, we were researching the history of this issue. The records of various news sources painted, what I believe (my personal opinion) is a clear picture of deceit, distortion, personal assassinations, dismissal of the people most affected and tunnel vision, with but one goal in mind, come what may. I would ask," if supposedly honorable people knowingly do dishonorable deeds, are they still honorable?"

"Here is some of the new information that we found regarding this issue: I know this sounds like the same information already in the "book" but as the days go by, we find more stories with information we were unaware of and a new picture is emerging, "one that is very troubling and affects all Americans".

2001: two NCAA Committees (Minority Opportunities and Interests Committee (MOIC) and the Executive Subcommittee on Gender Diversity Issues) issue a recommendation against the Confederate Flag being display at NCAA Executive controlled sporting events and then adds Native Americans to that recommendation.

2005 Myles Brand announces a new NCAA policy to ban Native American names and imagery from NCAA tournaments and post season play.

What brought this about? Evidently a handful of Native Americans complained and are being used to justify the two committee's recommendation to eliminate Native Americans from view. (My opinion) Little if any is mentioned of the elites within the University system (who are not Indians) or NCAA Executive System and their supposed reason. Who are these people? As I said in the beginning of this book, I cannot read minds, but I form opinions based on actions. I truly believe there are people who can only feel relevant through creating turmoil. I also believe there are those who believe they are smarter than anyone else, therefore those that do not agree must be silenced. But it appears as though the NCAA did not try to find out or even care what the majority of Native Americans felt, when adopting

89

the new policy, but instead sought out and only used voices that agree with them and their opinion is (in my opinion): That Native Americans are "Hostile and Abusive".

2006 NCAA Executive Committee: Exempts a number of Universities from their new policy on the approval of the closest namesake tribe. (There were threats of lawsuits.)

April, 2006 - Walter Harrison, Chairman of the NCAA executive committee, (NPR NEWS) when faced with conflicting statements, the NCAA made (what I consider) a convenient choice, with statements in hand from an opposition leaders as well as two supporters. He chooses to reject anything from supporters and except at "face value" the opposition statement. He states that Ron His Horse is Thunder's letter was the deciding factor. He rejects Archie Fool Bear's letter, District representative from Standing Rock as well as the UND President's, statement. Apparently, the NCAA has no interest in what the people felt or the truth or is there some other motive?

On Oct., 2006 in district court, (Northeast Central Judicial District) "an affidavit by Dr. Bernard Franklin "swears" Ron His Horse is Thunder's letter dated April 27, 2006 was a factor.

November 2006, State of North Dakota, by and through the North Dakota State Board of Higher Education, and the University of North Dakota, officially file the Lawsuit against the NCAA.

No one questions motives of the opponent, but are quick to label supporters as Racist, Bigots, Elitists, etc., but a process had begun, which will lead to the Settlement/Agreement of Oct, 2007. But clearly most North Dakotans are fighting to save the name and logo at this point in time. Was our Attorney General? It has been said that the Engelstad Foundation put up a million dollars to fight the NCAA. Attorneys were sought, but Attorney General Wayne Stenehjem, said he has jurisdiction on this issue and took the lead. He brings a suit against the NCAA Executive_Committee's authority to adopt the new policy and he states "this is not about the name and logo, but about the committee's authority" (page 13 of the original lawsuit from 2006).

On July 1ˢᵗ, 2007 William Goetz became the new Chancellor of the ND State Board of Higher Education and on July 2, 2007 it is reported that he met with the NCAA on the issue at the Minneapolis airport.

Early September, 2007, movement begins between North Dakota Attorney General's office and the NCAA. The trial date has been set for December 10ᵗʰ, 2007 and North Dakota is in a great legal position.

Most observers including the Attorney General believe North Dakota has almost no chance of losing in court, but for some reason the Attorney General negotiates a Settlement/Agreement with the NCAA and on Oct 26, 2007. The Settlement is signed by the ND State Board of Higher Education after the recommendation from the Attorney General. Why?

The Settlement/Agreement has also shifted focus from NCAA Executive Committees Authority to now focusing on the Sioux people. Why?

Oct.29, 2007 Bernard Franklin "Senior Vice President for Governance and Membership at the NCAA", states (First amendment center) "*the **Sioux people** and no one else should decide whether and how their name should be used*".

What has changed since that statement and Why? Is it because the Sioux people of North Dakota do not agree with the NCAA position, that they no longer are important to the NCAA and their voice, now must not be heard?

January 13ᵗʰ, 2008 NCAA Convention where the Executive Committee had promised to get the authority to adopt such a policy, but instead refuses to state what they seek (Minutes from NCAA Convention January 8ᵗʰ, 2008) and only gets clarification of the NCAA Executive Committee's current authority, the amendment does not increase power or give legislative power to the Executive Committee. When asked to give an example of what the amendment will do, no explanation is forth coming. "Why" is it because the NCAA Executive Committee's true intentions must be kept a secret and with the Settlement/Agreement there is no need to risk exposure of true intentions?

Also in January 2008 Chancellor Goetz eliminates any opportunity for North Dakotans or even the ND State Board of Higher Education input for the new President of UND, by giving only one choice "his choice".

July 2008: The new President of UND assumes the post. He states he and his Administration well remain neutral on this.

Oct 4, 2008 & Oct 9th (courtesy of the Grand Forks Herald), Gordon Caldis, an elderly attorney and alumni of UND, he asks the board to reconsider Settlement/Agreement and return to court, *Oct.9, 2008.* Even though the NCAA Executive Committee still does not have authority, the ND State Board rejects Gordon's proposal, stating, " he is a very nice man with the best of intentions, but he's mistaken". Attorney General Wayne Stenehjem stated in 2006 "the lawsuit was not about the name and logo, but about NCAA Executive Committee's authority".

WHY and WHO decided to change the direction in the Settlement/Agreement and does not the January 2008 NCAA Convention outcome give reason to return to court?

January 9th, 2009 Grand Forks Herald: Will Summit decision speed things up?   Summit League is a new obstacle brought into the mix and becomes a big distraction. Why and who started the talks while a court agreement is pending?

January 11, 2009 Grand Forks Herald Editorial, Opinion section, Mike Jacobs, "It's completely clear that the Sioux do object to the name and logo" (not true) He goes on" Even if there were a vote, the result could not be guaranteed, of course, because they could later change their minds". I thought to myself "what"? You should not be allowed to vote because you might change your mind later! This is the most stupid remark I have ever heard concerning "voting rights" and this comes from a supposedly educated man.

February 10, 2009 Grand Forks Herald, Tu-Uyen Tran: "Tribal members want nickname on ballot": Chairwoman Myra Pearson, indicates she personally opposes nickname, but can't speak for the whole tribe but she would support a tribal wide vote. Chancellor Goetz does not think a referendum will be enough. Goetz also said he sought

two more committee members for a board set up in January to meet
with the tribes on the nickname issue. (We are still waiting.)

February 22, 2009: the one and the only open meeting of the so-
called UND committee takes place and listens to Spirit Lake
opposition leader Erich Longie which he states "that they can only
meet with the Tribal Government and not the Tribal members"; this
comes after Committee Chairman Grant Shaft suggests visiting with
tribal members. They must agree because no meet ever takes place and
tribal members are rejected from that point on.

March 4, 2009 Grand Forks Herald, Amy Dalrymple: UND
nickname receives more 'pro-logo' criticism. At the ND State Board
Committee meeting, Erich Longie from Spirit Lake states "In my
opinion, the makeup of the committee and the work they're doing is
close to unethical and immoral" and Leigh Jeanotte said, "The makeup
on the committee looks like it's aiming to retain the logo." What do
they want, nothing but the opposition there? They pretty much have it
any way through the leadership of the ND State Board committee, but
in the Settlement it does state "seek and obtain support".

March 6, 2009 Grand Forks Herald, Tu-Uyen Tran: Nickname
prompts two petitions: Again the false accusations make their way
into the story "Longie (Erich) said he feels that the supporters are
working on behalf of the Engelstad family foundation. If outside
interests can circumvent the Tribal Council with impunity, he reasons,
that undermines tribal sovereignty." He also states, "He's actually glad
there may be a vote, because it takes pressure off the Tribal Council."
Again false, if he truly felt that way, why does he challenge the Tribal
Council in court April 16, 2009 trying to stop a vote?

April 2, 2009 Grand Forks Herald, Tu-Yuen Tran "Nickname
divides UND Senate". The UND senate adopts a resolution opposing
the name and logo. It was opposed unanimously by student senators,
but was passed by faculty and staff. Vice Chairwoman Wendelin
Hume refused to say who sponsored the resolution. *Was this at the
direction of the administration? Where is this so-called neutral
position?*

April 9, 2009 Grand Forks Herald, Tu-Yuen Tran: Sioux tribes
begin nickname campaigns: Almost the entire article is dedicated to
93

the opposition's viewpoint. Contrary to reports, our committee focused on getting out the vote, not on how to vote. *We were and are willing to except the will of the tribal members.* We did not put any presentation on telling people how to vote. Just to vote! Unlike the opposition who, put presentation on though out the reservation (I attended one), they served lunch, handed out fliers that were made up on a computer, probable by "a 5 year" old kid, they suggest all frat party's focus on Native Americans, they presented as fact, where the fliers originated to tribal members. When in fact they, told reporter Tran of the Grand Forks Herald, they did not know.

April 15, 2009, Grand Forks Herald, Kevin Fee: University of South Dakota, announces Summit League acceptance: The story is about after the 2010-11 season. UND will not play South Dakota in sports, unless it joins the Summit League also. South Dakota will join the league in sports in July of 2011. What is overlooked in the story is the fact that the Settlement/Agreement will end Nov. 30, 2010. Everything would be settled one way or another 9 months before UND would be able to take the field of play. What's the hurry?

April 17, 2009 Devils Lake Journal: Where it all comes from: Interview from the 16th, with Amy Phillips. As she spoke to enrolled members at Spirit Lake on April 16 among some of her words were, "It embarrasses me that you are put in this position" and"I'm embarrassed that a predominantly white University...has put this strife and tension on you". She also states that she and her husband have researched the name and logo over the past 80 years and supplied the various logos. She fails to mention, why the changes happened or the respect that prompted those changes. I thought she stated earlier that she was new to all of this? Now she and her husband have some years experience? This sounds to me like getting rid of names and images is, "a passion of hers".

April 18, 2009, Grand Forks Herald, Tu-Uyen Tran : Nickname struggle intensifies: Erich Longie, said " he's not clear just who produced the fliers, but he doesn't disavow its use" the justification, " Erich Longie, it's not whether Engelstad said what the fliers claim-- it's the necessity of such tactics when fighting from a weak position." As Tran writes in his "City Beat" the toughest story, when Erich pressed on tactics, Tran writes "I realized what he was trying to say was, in effect, the end justifies the means".

94

April 18, 2009 Grand Forks Herald, Tu-yuen Tran: Pride and prejudice drive tribal nickname debate: Although this article is (in my opinion) the fairest to date, it still gave more coverage to opposition's point of view. It also states, that both sides are trying to persuade voters. That is not true. Our committee has not put on even one presentation, to persuade members on how to vote. Unlike the opposition who have put on numerous presentations throughout the reservation, with the aid of UND staff. Our committee only worked for the people's right to vote and now encourage them to vote.

*April 21, 2009,*Grand Forks Herald, Tom Disselhorst, Bismarck, letter: Nickname settlement was imposed on tribes: He basically says, that the tribes were not parties to the agreement and tribal leaders oppose the name, so retire the name and logo. He overlooks the fact that when the agreement is read, one can only come to the conclusion, that is this, the Sioux people will determine the outcome. If retired, the Sioux people will be blamed, whenever it is retired.

April 21, 2009, Grand Forks Herald, Archie Ingersoll: Kelly distances UND from tribal decisions on Fighting Sioux nickname: Kelly said, "I will emphasize that the university does not interfere in the workings of sovereign nations". Did he not know about Amy Philips and all the other UND staff comments or of statements to come in the next two days? Was this statement only to give a false picture?

April 21, 2009, Grand Forks Herald, Tu-Yuen Tran: Spirit Lake votes overwhelmingly support   the Fighting Sioux nickname: 774 "yes" to 378 "no" or 67% in support. Again, the story is filled with opposition views and suggesting they are victims of the REA.

April 22, 2009, Grand Forks Herald, Tu-Yuen Tran: Unknowns remain after nickname vote: "Many issues are still up in the air despite a decisive vote." Much of the story is about the opposition's intentions, very little on the positive side. There were a number of statements from State Board member Grant Shaft, none of which were encouraging.

May 3, 2009 Grand Forks Herald, Erich Longie Viewpoint: We'll never give up anti-nickname fight: "I want to be very clear about this. Davidson does not speak for me and the 371 tribal members who voted against the logo". He goes on to say," He's trying to prevent outside organization coming on to the reservation and unfairly influencing an election", I want to be very clear about this, my thoughts were "Erich Longie does not speak for me or the 774 (67%) of enrolled members that voted in support of the logo and let me further say, once again Erich, you are the only one that has brought in outside influences."

May13th, 2009 Grand Forks Herald; Summit League "intervening issue" the story is about the need to hurry because of Summit League. The Board may retire name and logo at the next meeting. The story gave the impression the Summit League is opposed to the name and image, which is again misleading. The Summit League only wants the issue resolved, which is later stated by the Commissioner of the Summit League.

CHAPTER 10:
A NEW STRATEGY IS NEEDED

May 16, 2009, (Courtesy of Grand Forks Herald): "Higher Ed board weighs opportunities, cost of UND nickname change." It is suggested; the cost of retiring the name and image will run at the very least $ 750,000.00. (which they later claim not to have any idea) UND hopes to join the Summit League. The Summit League is a stronger league and fits our needs." It's the only one; there is no interest in the Big Sky League, at this time. Travel time and cost is a big concern. "

There are three interesting things in this story that will eventually show what we believe is more deceit and a common practice of the State Board of Higher Education, President Kelly and the NCAA. It will all become clear later.

It was becoming clear as the summer rolled on, that Standing Rock was probably not going to get a vote in time. We at Spirit Lake were being totally minimized and ignored. It was as if we did not exist or were not considered Indians. All the focus was on Standing Rock, one would expect some mention of Spirit Lake, but the Grand Forks Herald stories were very misleading (in our opinion) and focused strictly on Standing Rock and their Tribal Council overlooking how the Tribal member's rights were being denied.

There was a battle going on at Standing Rock which the press seemed to have taken sides on. To read the paper one would have the impression that almost all members of Standing Rock openly oppose the name and logo, but from what we heard from Archie and others, if they get a vote it will be the same results if not more in support than Spirit Lake.

In every story, the Herald had to include, "The NCAA feels Native American Name's and Imagery are hostile and abusive" and that the Settlement/Agreement requires both tribe's approval. Almost no mention of the fact that Standing Rock's enrolled members have been trying for years to have their voice heard, which led to the many resolutions passed by the Tribal Council to silence Tribal members.

The Herald also keeps reprinting the "30" year requirement, as if it were in the original Settlement/Agreement, which it was not! They continually avoid printing the total true facts. They had to know that the ND State Board of Higher Education violated the Settlement/Agreement when they added the "30" year requirement without getting written agreement from the NCAA as required in the Settlement/Agreement on page 9, lines 5, (Modifications in Writing). Any modifications to this Agreement must be in writing and executed by University of North Dakota and the NCAA. They also violated the spirit of the agreement which said that UND had 3 years to seek and obtain approval from the two tribes. As I have said, it did not "say seek out opposition" and aid them in their efforts, which is what they did (intentionally or not).

To believe that all (NCAA Executive Committee, ND State Board of Higher Education, University of North Dakota, Attorney General's office and the Herald) knew nothing of what each other was doing is in my estimation unbelievable! I believe it is and has been a coordinated effort.

But that is where we are at in mid-summer of 2009 and by the end of July we knew that Charlie Murphy and Ron His Horses Thunder were the two candidates for Standing Rock tribal chairman. Charlie was the only candidate through the primary campaign that said he would work to have the people's voice heard if elected. In the July primary Ron His Horses Thunder came in second and Avis Little Eagle came in third, one vote behind Ron. Their total vote combined was less than Charlies. We had life again or so we thought. If Charlie won the general election as it appeared he would, we thought the members of Standing Rock would finally be able to speak.

But there was still the deadline date that would have to be overcome. At the State Board meeting in May 14, 2009, the deadline date had been suggested as Aug. 1, 2009 but was agreed to by the Board of Sept. 15, 2009 (May 14, 2009, Board minutes). Because the General election was not until mid-September, they changed it to Oct. 1, 2009. The general election was then delayed until Sept. 30, 2009, so the Board changed it to Oct. 15, 2009.

(I believe) the Board knew the general election date from the beginning, because of their admitted close contact with Ron His Horses Thunder and they were also aware he said Standing Rock will never have a vote as long as he was chairman at Standing Rock. The dates were set knowing that even if Charlie were elected he would not have time to get anything accomplished as far as the Settlement/Agreement requirements were concerned. Then, there was always the talk of the Summit League and a need to hurry.

The general election did finally happen on Sept. 30, 2009 and Charlie won easily, but Charlie was not able to officially take the seat of chairman until Oct. 15, 2009, but even then they still had to fill his old seat on the Council before anything could really be done.

It was public pressure that made the Board change the date to Nov. 1, 2009, and finally until Nov. 30, 2009. There were constant negative stories in the Herald, especially when any important event was coming up. Again it is our opinion that they were always trying to affect the outcome.

Not knowing what was actually happening on Standing Rock, only from the communications from Archie, who has faith in Charlie. But from the day Charlie was announced the winner, pressure from the ND State Board of Higher Education was immediately put on him to act "right now". The Grand Forks Herald told the stories of Chancellor Goetz's numerous letters to Charlie, about the need to hurry and the "30" year agreement. Charlie responded a couple of times about how his old seat had to be filled first and later he said that he was just elected and the tribe has many pressing issue, we need some time, he also responded with a letter to Chancellor Goetz in which he said there was a need to meet and talk about the whole thing.

But by the end of August 2009, we on Spirit Lake were getting worried again, time was running out and as a committee we put word out that we needed legal help, but had no money. Pat Morley, a North Dakota attorney and alumni of UND answered the plea for help and offered to represent us Pro-Bono.

We met a number of times with Mr. Pat Morley to explore our options in September of 2009. Pat told us it was going to be difficult to force the State Board to follow the Settlement/Agreement. The NCAA and Board did a good job of putting the Sioux in the middle and still make us more or less meaningless.

The biggest problem for us to overcome was going to be "we were not a party to the agreement" and they would be claiming we don't have "Standing" although we are the center point.

(Courtesy of Tu-Uyen Tran and Grand Forks Herald), Sept. 11, 2009: Down To the Wire: The article talks about the need for the "30" year agreement, but they may need to move the Oct. 1 deadline.

(Courtesy of Tu-Uyen Tran and Grand Forks Herald), Sept. 16, 2009: Spirit Lake issues nickname resolution: in the article is an interview with one of the opposition leaders on Spirit Lake who is the son of the Spirit Lake Tribal Chairwoman. In it, he states the only thing the resolution says is that the council confirms there was a vote. It does not give support.

What is not mentioned in the story is that the resolution as reported was not what the council voted on and that when they found out their resolution was changed after their vote they were angry. They had voted to give 100 years on the resolution. But the Tribal Chair and tribal secretary changed the wording from what was voted on and unanimously approved by the only ones authorized to speak on the issue "the Tribal Council".

(Courtesy of Tu-Uyen Tran and Grand Forks Herald), Sept. 17, 2009: Nickname supporters and opponent speak about Oct. 1 deadline to the State Board: The article is mainly from the opposing point of view and how the resolution is meaningless. Erich Longie talked about the lack of education of those that support the name and image on the reservation.

(Courtesy of Tu-Uyen Tran and Grand Forks Herald), Sept. 18, 2009: Spirit Lake's new resolution approves 'perpetual' use of the name and logo: (resolution # A05-09-191). State Board member Grant Shaft says a binding agreement is needed. He is indicating that a signed contract by the two tribes guaranteeing they will give up all rights on this issue.

Two-thirds of the article is from the negative points. By now it was not only crystal clear to us, but cemented in our souls; we were indeed fighting the NCAA, the North Dakota State Board of Higher Education and the University of North Dakota, President and his Administration as well as some professors at UND and the Grand Forks Herald.

What my husband saw clearly months ago, but we did not want to believe was true. "There was and is an intentional effort by these groups to change the name and logo and blame the Sioux for it". They have used a small handful of Native Americans that for whatever reason did not want the name to stay and would do anything to get rid of it and they had joined forces with the devil to do it. They even turned against their own relatives and tribal people.

(Courtesy of Tu-Uyen Tran and Grand Forks Herald) Nov. 9, 2009: Judge Orders State Board to delay UND nickname decision: But it had been finally agreed to. We are now trying the courts. On November 9, 2009 we submitted a petition for a temporary restraining order against the State Board in Ramsey County District Court (case # 09-C-00419). The worst that could happen we might delay the Board for enough time for Standing Rock to have a vote. The best would be we would finally get some respect on this issue. The state citizens would realize it's not the "Sioux people" but the elitists in the education systems that are actually causing all the turmoil. (my opinion)

Nov. 17, 2009: Our attorney Pat Morley sends an e-mail to now President Mr. Emery of the NCAA stating "Spirit Lake People vs. State Board of Higher Education" in which he asks the NCAA on behalf of the Committee for Understanding and Respect to request the State Board to follow the agreement. No response was received that we are aware of.

A hearing date was set for December 9, 2009 in Ramsey County District Court. The ND State Board could not act before the hearing. Just as we suspected, the Grand Forks Herald was quick to get the stories in the paper about how we had "No Standing in the Agreement" and the case should be dismissed (this was before we even went to court).

Because of the Summit League, there was a need to hurry the hearing, so the court case was scheduled sooner than normal and on December 9, 2009, the court did convene.

With all the distortion and "so called" expert opinions in the Grand Forks Herald, it is a wonder that we made it to court, but another big day had arrived. It was decided that John Chaske would speak for the committee. Present at the hearing were, among others myself and my husband, John Chaske, Frank Black Cloud, Renita Delorme, Lavonne Alberts, Demus McDonald, Alex Yankton and Jody Hodgson, Earl Strinden and Gorden Caldis. On the other side was Assistant Attorney General Doug Barr, Grant Shaft, Chancellor Goetz, President Kelly and other ND State Board members.

Because of a conflict of interest by local judges, the judge had to come from Rugby, 60 miles away. But the court was called to order and attorneys from both sides said they were ready to proceed.

Pat Morley's opening statement started by showing the "80" year history of respect and honor shown by the University and the REA. He played 2 video's showing the honor that the REA bestowed before each hockey game.

Doug Barr Assistant Attorney General and representing the board objected to this presentation on the grounds that it was not relevant, but it was over ruled. Pat presented the official vote tally from Spirit Lake in which 67% of the members voiced support for the name and logo. He presented the Agreement in which it called for UND and the Board "to seek support" and that the Agreement gives till November 30, 2010 and that anyway you read it the Sioux are the center point.

Doug Barr's opening statement was to indicate the "Sioux" were not and are not part of the Agreement; thereby they have no standing in the court on this issue. Furthermore, individual members can not

102

show any benefits or damages and cannot speak for the tribe. This case should be dismissed. The judge allowed the hearing to continue.

Pat Morley called John Chaske to the stand and asked him, "As a spiritual leader, what does the ceremony from 1969 mean?" John explained that under our customs and traditions, that once something is given and the sacred pipe is used, it cannot be taken back. Then John was asked what the name means to the people of Spirit Lake? He explained how proud we are to have our ancestors connected to such a fine University and the educational opportunities it gives our people and that it keeps us relevant in today's world. John was then asked how retirement of the name would affect the tribe? He responded with, "As a people we would be more isolated in the future and that the educational opportunities at UND, probably would be the first cut under financially difficult times." Doug Barr didn't have any questions for John, so he was excused.

Closing statements were then presented. First was Doug Barr and he proceeded to argue that the agreement does not require the Board to wait till the deadline to change the name. That they can change the name and logo anytime they want. That the tribes were not a party to the agreement and have no say, they have no standing.

Then Pat Morley presented our closing argument. He pointed out the "Sioux" were named many times in the agreement, thereby making them a third party beneficiary. That to terminate the agreement early would damage the tribes, that the loss of the name would further isolate the tribes, that it could damage education for tribal members.

The whole hearing took about 45 minutes with the judge asking a number of questions. He was sure that no matter what his decision was going to be, there would be an appeal and due to the time factor he would render his decision by the end of the month. Court was adjourned.

December 18th, 2009: the judge issues his opinion which does not surprise us but it does disappoint us. In remarks he says that he reluctantly came to the decision, but there is nothing in the Settlement that forbids early retirement. Although the Tribes have limited "Standing" because of their mention, the North Dakota State of Higher

Education under the ND Constitution has the authority to control the name and image.

Now we have to decide if we are going to appeal. It is an easy call for us on the committee, but Pat Morley points out a few things that could happen. One being there is a possibility that court costs could be assessed if the North Dakota Supreme Court would even hear the case. On February 12th, 2010 our attorney submitted the appeal and the date for the hearing was set for March 23rd, 2010. The injunction although not forbidding the ND State Board of Higher Education from proceeding on retirement, was never really addressed and made early retirement an uncomfortable decision for the State board.

The day of the Supreme Court arguments Pat Morley was laid up from back surgery and his associate Lolita Romanick would present our arguments. Although we had never met her and saw her for the first time only moments before the court convened we were pleasantly surprised with her abilities in the court room. It was clear that the law firm had prepared her for the argument in court. But again Doug Barr said we are meaningless and have no standing, that the North Dakota Constitution gives unlimited power to the State Board and they can change any name for any reason at any time and that the 2007 Settlement/Agreement in no way forces them to wait till the deadline date before retiring the name.

The court asked many questions and seemed very sympathetic to our cause and dilemma. They wanted to know why the tribes were not included in talks before the Settlement/Agreement was signed. They pointed out that the committee represents 67% of the enrolled members of the tribe because of our efforts in getting the vote, which gives the committee Limited Standing.

April of 2010: the North Dakota Supreme Court ruled as we feared. Although we lost in the court we had accomplished the least of our goals by stopping the State Board from retiring the name and logo for the last 6 months. Sadly, Standing Rock members had not been able to take advantage of the extra time, due to the Tribal Council.

Now we are wondering just what our next step should be if any. We had traveled a long and winding road to get here and we seemed to be at a dead end. In the last 30 months there have been so many twists and turns, so many times we climb the mountain and felt like we were on top of the world only to be pushed off the side of a cliff. We had done what was asked of us only to be ridiculed and slandered. At every triumph new obstacles were placed before us.

Do we still have the will to go on? Is there any place to even go? What else could even be done? It really looked like the end had arrived and all our efforts had been for nothing. We are <u>just Indians to the establishment.</u>

Chapter 11:
Fall Out Through Hot Air

The more we find out about the whole process that has taken place here in North Dakota, the more our stomachs churned. I am actually getting sick to my stomach and my heart is breaking, because of these people who think what they want gives them the right to destroy the entire tribe and its members as well as a once proud University. The only crime the enrolled members of Spirit Lake committed was to feel proud of their heritage and they did what was asked of them. The tiny groups with tiny minds are on a campaign to destroy the name and logo at any cost, and they have been aided by the Herald, (my opinion)

I actually got a case of Shingles out of the turmoil and needed sometime to myself, while John was going through the same thoughts. We had to question, "Why are we doing this and is it worth the trouble?" A few of the Committee members were just plain angry about how we had just been used and treated by "so-called" honorable people.

But as I said, in the summer of 2009 we were researching the history of the Fighting Sioux issue focusing as far back to 1930. We had found some interesting facts that the NCAA and UND Administration as well the ND State Board seemed to be relying on in their goal to rid UND of our name and image. All documents, letters, Ceremonies, and programs in support of the name and image were overlooked by these opposition groups or just dismissed as not important.

The ND State board was now relying on the same negative material, such as numerous resolutions and complaints that the NCAA used to deny UND its exemption. They were given full weight by the NCAA and now the ND State board also; resolutions of support were overlooked or twisted by the NCAA when the lawsuit was brought and now the ND State Board had joined the effort.

UND had the same support that was used in the case of numerous other Universities, who did receive their exemptions. The resolutions the NCAA relied on were signed by the same people over and over again, names such as; Charlie Murphy, David Gipp, Jesse Taken Alive, Ron His Horses Thunder and Tex Hall appear over and over dating back as far as 1999.

They put much stock in politically correct professors and their opinions disregarding the Sioux people themselves. Evidently, the NCAA as well as the politically correct professors feel Native Americans are too stupid to know what's good for them. A belief the elites have relied on for hundreds of years in the pursuit of personal goals.

The NCAA chooses to overlook the 1969 Ceremony which holds till the end of time, but the real clincher is the ND State Board members and the University of North Dakota officials knew as well as we did about the ceremony, and if they really wanted to keep the Sioux name and symbol at UND. All the ND State board had to do was hold the NCAA to their own standard of asking for one tribe as in other states that received exemption to save their name and logo.

The Spirit Lake Tribe gave their support in the 1969 Sacred Ceremony, again in a 2000 (resolution #A05-01-041) and a vote in 2009 and again in 2009 (resolution # A05-09-191) to use the name and logo at the University. It seems clear to me that the ND State Board kept using the 2007 Settlement/Agreement to cover up for them wanting the name and logo to be gone and to blame the Sioux for it!

The NCAA chooses to listen to hearsay rather than rely on provable facts. They choose to sit in their cushiony comfortable offices and sending communications to known opposition leaders "Asking if they would support the name and logo: (my opinion). Is this a real effort to find out the truth or just to find justification for a decision already made? As of yet, we supporters have never been contacted for input and believe this was and is intentional, or was the NCAA Executive Committee looking for something else?

Then you have the Office of Civil Rights that in 2001 found NO Evidence to a "hostile or abusive environment" to exist at UND. But the NCAA discarded that part of the evaluation and just focused on the Office of Civil Rights (opinion) opposing names and imagery.

But here we are fighting the UND Administration and the ND State Board of Higher Education supposedly because of the NCAA and the fear of the NCAA sanctions or are there other reasons.

(Courtesy of Grand Forks Herald Dec. 19, 2009), District Judge reluctantly dismisses nickname suit: Although he said we do have "Limited Standing", the North Dakota Constitution gives the ND State board the power to change any nickname at any time, for any reason and there is nothing in the Settlement/Agreement to prevent them from early retirement. My thought was if the ND State Board, knew this "why did they put the two tribes and the state of North Dakota into such turmoil if they had the authority to change the name all along anyway"? And they were going to do so anyway? My opinion the ND State board did not want to be the fall guy for changing The Fighting Sioux name and logo, but wanted to look like the good guy.

February 2010: We filed an appeal to the ND Supreme Court, which would be argued in March of 2010. Again because of the "Summit League", there was a need to hurry the process. Pat Morley told us that there would be no testimony given by individuals, only attorneys would speak.

Because of our injunction against the ND State board, word was getting out and the National press seemed to take notice of it also. A number of National news media and even one from Canada news outlets contacted us for interviews.

Because of the skepticism created by the Herald, we were concerned about what kind of coverage we would receive from these news outlets and we always asked before granting interviews, "Is this going to be truthful or slanted?" But here again, we were duped, after promising that our position and our point of views would be reported and nothing would be taken out of context, here again much truth was left out or minimized.

I believe it was in the summer of 2009 that a group of Native Americans out of Canada contacted us and wanted to get our views for a radio program that airs weekly in Canada. They promised it would be fair and unedited. We agreed to meet with them and met at the old museum where I worked. John, Renita DeLorme and I met with them for about 45 minutes and felt good that someone was going to get our side of the story out. But no surprise, when it aired, it was only a "5" minute segment and our side had just over a minute, but almost 4 minutes dedicated to why the name and image should go.

Then there was the New York Times and almost none of what we told them along with the proof to back it up was printed. We and our tribe were totally minimized.

Then Valerie Richardson of the Washington Times after interviewing us did her story on February 17th, 2010 and although it is and was the fairest to date, it still left out much of the facts we told her and minimized our side's size and the importance of what we reported. Again much was left out.

March 10th, 2010: We were at the N D Supreme Court hearing and again heard Assistant Attorney General Doug Barr, talk about how we had no "Standing" and the case should be dismissed. Again the court ruled against us, because under the North Dakota Constitution, the State Board has authority to change the name and logo, regardless of the Settlement/Agreement and there is nothing in the Settlement that prohibits early retirement. "Again I thought to myself, the only reason they haven't retired it was becoming clearer to me that they did want the Sioux of North Dakota to be blamed".

It was darn hard to sit and listen to all the twisted talk, the blaming of the Sioux for not giving our blessing, yet denying us the opportunity to do so. It was always, "It's the "Sioux's" fault and we need to join the Summit League or we will perish as a University", and then, add that the "Sioux" mean nothing, have no "Standing", don't listen to them, we at the State Board are the only ones to count and it's the NCAA's fault you know.

Members from Standing Rock and Spirit Lake along with many fans walking in support of keeping the Fighting Sioux name and symbol.

April 8th, 2010: The ND Supreme Court rules against us which didn't surprise us but very much disappointed us, but it didn't stop us, for just days later, one of our new "found friends" had scheduled a support walk in Grand Forks.

Danielle Sime (a Sioux supporter) had called me about a walk she had organized on the UND campus and was wondering if it would be something in which I would participate. Danielle who is an avid Fighting Sioux hockey fan had created a Facebook page (We the People of North Dakota Demand Answers Save Fighting Sioux) dedicated to the Fighting Sioux and was willing to do anything she could to help and did organize the walk that did take place on April 16th, 2010. It started about 5:00 PM with tribal members speaking as well as alumni before the walk, and it was after 10:00 PM when we finished for the night.

She was expecting around two hundred people, but it turned out to be much larger. Although the news media tried to down play the size of the rally and walk saying (depending on which news outlet the reports were from) 200 to 500 people, but in truth was that the 10 block walk had people at the starting point, when the leaders had reached the end of the walk. We estimated close to 1000 and then there were those in the buildings we passed that hung out the windows yelling support or the hundreds of cars driving up and down the street tooting their horns and yelling support "GO SIOUX"!!

There were members of our committee in attendance as well as Archie and some of his tribal members along with Native American students from the University there in support. But sadly the news media had to throw in their usual negative side talking, and about how much more police had to be there to make sure it stayed peaceful.

I'm not sure if it was before or after our rally the opposition also hand a rally at the Memorial Hall on campus, in which Clyde Belcourt and David Gipp were the facilitators. Their rally got much more coverage even though they only had about 50 people in attendance, there was no march and the event lasted about an hour.

But here we are in the spring of 2010, and finally the ND State board has gotten their wish and goal, nothing to stop them now and at the next Board meeting, they will officially retire the Name and Logo. They have avenged Custer and defeated the Sioux or so they thought.

From the early 1930's, when UND athletics had adopted the Sioux name for the University, they played with pride for over 80 years. Over the years, whenever us Sioux had objected to the imagery being portrayed as less than respectful ways, the University has address those issues, such as Sammy Sioux and followed the tribe's requests and made changes with our permission.

In 1969 leaders from Standing Rock and Spirit Lake as well as tribal members traveled to UND to perform a Sacred Ceremony, making the UND President an honorary chief of the tribe that would guarantee educational opportunities for our people in return for perpetual use of our likeness and name at UND. Also in 1969 the UND Indian Association was formed and UND has now the most Native American programs of any major University in the Nation. In the 1990's a handful of Native Americans with connections to AIM along with Social Works Professors at UND's Merrifield Hall started protesting. Also, a number of tribal governments passed resolutions opposing all the names and images. In most if not all cases without tribal member knowledge.

In 2000 Spirit Lake Tribal Council passed a resolution in support of the Name and Logo as long as something positive came out of it. They had the people's blessing. This was in response to those others outside the State resolutions.

111

2001 Ralph Engelstad stops construction on the new arena after investing over 25 million dollars because of indications the name will change. He is again guaranteed the name will stay.

In 2001, the Ralph Engelstad Arena was completed and opened its doors. The Arena had cost over 104 million dollars and was built by Mr. Engelstad with the guarantee that it would stay the Fighting Sioux.

Also in 2001 after complaints by UND professors and a handful of Native Americans, the Office of Civil Rights investigated UND and Grand Forks. It concluded that there was NO evidence in support of a Hostile or Abusive environment at UND or Grand Forks.

2002 Sports Illustrated takes a survey of Native Americans and finds 76% of those polled supported Native names and images.

2003 Pennsylvania's Annenberg election survey finds that 90% of Native Americans support names and images.

In 2005 Myles Brand, the President of the NCAA at the time adopted a policy from the Executive Committee against Native Americans. It is to take effect starting in 2006.

By 2006 the NCAA Executive Committee had exempted 8 of the 18 Universities from the policy. UND had the same qualifications as those 8, but was denied exemption by the NCAA Executive Committee. (Requirement: A namesake Tribes approval). This denial was based on Ron His Horses Thunders letter in which he states, that all Sioux oppose the name, Walter Harrison chairman of the Executive Committee rejects letters of Support in favor of His Horse's Thunder and denies UND's request for exemption.

October in 2006 North Dakota brought a lawsuit against the NCAA Executive Committee challenging their authority to adopt such policies.

April of 2007, the NCAA Executive Committee requests the District Court records of their communications to be sealed.

July of 2007 and a new Chancellor of the North Dakota State Board of Higher Education takes the helm, his name is William Goetz and he states he will be very involved with the Fighting Sioux issue. (We believe the focus change now is to get rid of the name and image) for he starts meeting with the NCAA.

September 24th, 2007, the District Court seals all communication records, including the State Attorney General's request for NCAA communication with the opposition and Forum Communications tries to un-seal those records through North Dakota Freedom of Information Act, but is denied access. (My opinion, The Court has either taken sides or the two sides agree with the court's decision).

October of 2007 the NCAA Executive Committee and ND State board agrees to a Settlement avoiding going to court in December of 2007. According to the State Attorney General, the NCAA Executive Committee realizes they will lose the upcoming case, but are going to get authority and our victory will be short lived. The Settlement/Agreement also just about guarantees UND will have to change its name (we believe).

October 26th, 2007 and Bernard Franklin Senior Vice President of the NCAA said, "The Settlement Confirms the Sioux People and no one else should decide whether and how their name should be used". My thoughts, he says the Sioux members, not the tribal councils.

February of 2008 a new President for UND is selected. There was only one name was given for consideration "instead of the normal three "and Robert Kelley's name is submitted by Chancellor Goetz for the ND State board to accept over objections by some Board members.

March 7, 2008 The Attorney General, Wayne Stenehjem states; we filed our lawsuit and provided some strong legal briefs that lead the NCAA to conclude our lawsuit had merit and that we were going to win. (Increased authority, Joseph Marks 3/7/2008 courtesy of Grand Forks Herald) My question, why was this statement needed? Was it justification for early retirement?

April 21st, 2009 as Spirit Lake votes in the largest turn out in tribal history 67% vote in favor of keeping the name at UND. Within minutes of the results being reported, staff at UND on the WDAZ-TV news, claim level headed people would agree with him in opposition to the name and logo.

113

April 27th, 2010, Buffalo News; Standing Rock members turn in a petition with 1004 names, calling for a voice on the Fighting Sioux issue, through an election process.

Throughout the time period between January of 2008 and April 2010; our committee had attempted to contact the ND State board, UND Administration and the NCAA on numerous occasions, for the opportunity to share our views. We received little or no response.

Through the summer of 2010, we had been talking to our local legislators, and by December of 2010 more legislators were showing interest in a possible law being introduced at the next session.

CHAPTER 12:
THE FOG BEGINS TO LIFT

Now it's time to finally get an understanding of what has taken place. The Summit League is at hand, nothing standing in the way. The date had been set. The Summit League Officials are going to tour the UND campus on November 1st, 2010 and announce the acceptance of UND into the Summit League Conference. We were going to play our old rivals again. We hadn't played our number 1 rival North Dakota State University (NDSU) (Bison) for a few years now. We would play for the Nickel Trophy (Indian head on one side and Bison on the other) again. We would also play South Dakota another old rivalry. Till now the Summit League was always stated as the best conference for UND. Travel time and cost would be the least expensive. Some of the old rivalries going back almost a hundred years would be revived. For these and other reasons, it is where we belong.

But on October 26th, 2010, three years to the date of the Settlement/Agreement signing, and only four days before the Summit League's visit to announce UND's acceptance. Out of the clear blue sky came the announcement by President Kelley and UND Administration that UND had now joined the Big Sky Conference. *Where the hell did this come from?*

The Big Sky has two Montana schools where we would have to travel all the way across our state and go half way across Montana to play, and these are the two closest schools in the Big Sky. Most are west coast teams in Oregon and California half way across the country. Most of the teams and schools are not even known by North Dakotans.

What happened to playing the important rivalries that would fill the stands? The travel costs for Summit League would be at a minimum, it is "seventy eight" miles between UND and NDSU and it is only "three hundred and twenty one" miles to Sioux Falls, then it is "five hundred" mile to Omaha, Nebraska, the farthest travel we would make in the Summit League .

The Summit League never said they were opposed to the name and image, just that they wanted the issue resolved before considering our application. Was the Summit League only a diversion to give justification to get rid of the name before the Settlement date? Why the masquerade of trying to save the name and logo? Why has the State Board been fighting the only ones able to save the name? Can it be they did not want the name and image, but didn't dare to take credit for changing the name and image? *Why?*

But for the Big Sky, it's almost 600 miles to the Montana schools, and they are the close ones. The travel time and expense will more than double in the Big Sky and we will not play old rivals. This was not making sense to us or anyone else. Or is it because of our continued efforts, a new distraction was needed. *That new distraction did in fact, come, in the form of Big Sky President Doug Fullerton and plays a large part in the upcoming battles.*

Then, what about the NCAA? They had said it's up to the Sioux people; they couldn't help but know Standing Rock members were being held hostage and that Spirit Lake gave overwhelming support and the Sioux of North Dakota had even asked for their help, only to be rejected by them. Were we no longer important, *or was there a different motive?*

But during this time (2010) we had been talking to our legislator's throughout the late summer and fall. It seemed there was interest in passing a law on the Fighting Sioux name and logo. I guess the word was getting out that we Sioux had not given up yet, and we were encouraged by this and we might have life again.

With our face book page, *"We the People Demand Answers"*, *"Fighting Sioux Forever"* and other forms of the social media, we were getting the truth out, regardless of the local biased news coverage that was mostly controlled by Forum Communications. We knew through our face book page and talking to people, there was still a lot of support around the state for the name and logo and now some politicians were coming on board. It first started with one of our local Representatives, Dennis Johnson of the State legislature, and on to others throughout the State.

I had known Dennis Johnson for some time now because I use to work with his wife at Four Winds High School. The first time I met Dennis, I was working as school secretary, and Dennis came in from working on the farm and I assumed he was wondering about work, so I asked him to fill out a job application and he just lead me on till he finally told me who he was, and that he was there to see his wife. We had a good laugh after things were straightened out.

Dennis called and talked to me and said that another Representative would give me a call and ask about bringing a House Bill to save the Fighting Sioux name and logo. Shortly on that same day Representative Dave Munson gave me a call to find out how our committee would feel about this? I told him I would more than support it but had to talk with the rest of the committee from Spirit Lake. I did talk with other members of the committee and all supported the effort.

I believe it was around November of 2010 when I received a call from Representative Al Carlson, majority leader of the ND State House of Representatives. Although he is a graduate of NDSU he supports the UND Fighting Sioux and has been keeping watch on the issue and he was disgusted with how it has played out. He was wondering what my thoughts were on the possibility of a North Dakota law that would call for the UND Fighting Sioux and would I and the committee supports such an effort? After talking to committee members, they were all in agreement and we had life again. After discussing it with the committee I suggested we get hold of Jody Hodgson at the Ralph Engelstad Arena, since this issue impacted them also, and after speaking with Jody he said they'd be more than happy to attend and give testimony on this issue.

In December of 2010, it was pretty much set that in the January sessions of the legislature at least one law would be proposed. We would have to testify to the legislators on the Education Committee

CAPITAL IN BISMARCK, ND, MORNING OF TESTIMONY

and need to work on statements by all that were willing to address the legislators.

Here I go again; I'm way out of my elements. What was I going to say? What could I say that hadn't already been said? Then it dawned on me, these people had not gone through what the committee and I had for the last three years. They did not know what had really happened. Many of them probably didn't even know where Spirit Lake is.

Thank God, my husband had been saving so much information from newspapers as well as recording TV news stories. Over the last 3 years we would laugh at him because he was always bringing out his binders, which by now had grown to a large box of binders, but that information was helpful in preparing our statements as well as writing this book.

But here we go again, back into action and although all of us are getting very tired, we can't give up and abandon our people who

118

support this issue and our elders. What had started out just simply doing what had been asked of us has now turned into fighting for our honor and dignity.

We are about to meet old and new friends and colleagues that will join the fight, again without any knowledge of just what we are getting into. On January 25th, 2011 the day before the House Education Committee hearing, we met at the Kelly Inn in Bismarck, although we were staying at the Days Inn.

Some of the old friends to join us were Jody Hodgson, Earl Stinden, Archie Fool Bear, John Chaske, Lavonne Alberts, Renita DeLorme, and Gordon Caldis (who we had received books on the issue from). There were new friends that were to play a large part in the upcoming battles; Attorney Reed Soderstom, who had been working hard with Archie on Standing Rock, Sean Johnson, Kris Casement, Linus End of the Horn, Diane Gates, just to mention a few. The new friends were mainly alumni of UND.

We had rented one of the conference rooms at the Kelley Inn and our meeting began at six PM but first Representative ReAnn Kelch. She informed us of just how tomorrows hearing would go. She spoke about how to address the committee and that each side would have 90 minutes to present their case. First would be we supporters followed by a neutral position, then the opposition. Because of the time limit, we should try not to be to repctitive in our remarks. With that she said she could not stay for our rehearsal, it would be un-ethical and wished us well as she left.

Jody took charge of the meeting and suggested we do a dry run of our presentations. He suggested that we make our statements as brief as possible so as to get as many as we could in the limited time frame.

Jody started it off with his presentation about the 80 years of honored tradition and the respect paid to the Sioux at not just the REA but the whole University. His presentation lasted about 12 minutes and another "3" minute video. Which would be followed by Earl, then Gordon Caldis who were not at the rehearsal, but each would take about 10 minutes. They would be followed by John for another 10 minutes. Archie was up next and although he didn't have a prepared statement he spoke for a little over 10 minutes. Then Kris spoke for another 7 minutes followed by me for 12 minutes. Then Diane Gates for 7 minutes followed by Dave for 10 minutes and we were over the "90" minute time limit with more people to speak. We figured we would go as long as they would let us and added the rest to our list. We would see how it went in the morning and adjourned for the night.

The next morning as we sat having breakfast in the motel restaurant, Earl, Gordon and Jody were seated a few tables away from David, myself, John and Lavonne. Jody came over with the Minot Newspaper, all excited about a news story. On the front page was a big story about the Summit League.

The story was about a statement released from President Douple of the Summit League saying how he was pressured by the UND Administration and members of the State Board to come out against the name and Logo over the past two years. Wow, proof of what we had been saying for the last two years. *My thought was; apparently the President of the Summit League recognized that he and the League had been used as a pawn in a deceitful scheme just as we "Sioux" have been.*

As we left the motel heading for the capital building we were nervous to say the least, but still excited over the story in the paper. As we entered the conference room at the capitol we were told to sign in if we wanted to address the committee and it would be in the order of signing in.

First up was the individual's sponsoring the bills, there were three bills in all and after they had been introduced they were followed by legislators either for or opposed. It all took about half an hour. Then it was our turn.

As I said Jody was up first and talked about the honor displayed by UND for 80 years and that the Office of Civil Rights did an investigation in 2001 which found no evidence to support the allegations of "hostile or abusive" environment to exist at UND.

Then came Attorney Reed Soderstum and he talked about the Standing Rock Constitution and how it was and is being violated by the current Tribal Council. He added about Treaty rights and how they connect to the 1969 Sacred Ceremony.

He was followed by Earl Strinden talking about the REA and Ralph Engelstad, and just how he was guaranteed that the name and logo would stay at the University, this was to get a 104 million "dollar" facility built on campus.

Gordon Caldis was next and he presented evidence that there really is no adopted NCAA policy towards Native American names and imagery.

We had already eaten up 50 minutes of our allotted time and had many waiting to speak. I was getting worried but also relieved that there probably would not be time for me. As I looked around the room, it was filled, but not ever having attended one of these sessions before I thought nothing of it.

But now John was up and he did a great job of presenting a true picture of Spirit Lake members and just how important the name and logo are to our people, also as a spiritual leader just how significant the 1969 Ceremony is regarding our religious rights.

Then came Archie with information of how the Standing Rock Constitution is supposed to work. He added how it had been modified illegally but no courts would touch it, because of sovereignty issues, that the former Tribal attorney wrote an opinion that the modification was illegal. He also talked about investigating some of the allegations made against UND and Grand Forks, but could find no official reports ever filed. By the time he was done our time had just about run out.

The daughter of Edward Loon, Diane Gates, spoke about her father who was Standing Rock's traditional leader in 1969 and his support for the name at UND as well as the Ceremony he performed at that time.

The Chairperson of the House Education Committee, ReAnn Kelch looked around the room and announced what was clearly evident. She stated that normally we have maybe 15 people attending these sessions, but there are over 100 now. This is too important to follow timelines and that everybody will have their chance to speak if we had to go to mid-night. I got nervous again, I was going to have my chance to speak and it was now.

As I went to the podium to address the committee, my knees were shaking, I was not looking forward to this, but I had no choice. As instructed, I addressed the committee formally and began to speak. As I spoke the nervousness left me.

I started off with what the name and logo meant to me and went on to how we had polled the tribe before the referendum was even put on the ballot in 2009. How our people felt after voting only to have the State Board reject them. How we have pride in our elders and ancestors.

After me came Kris Casement talking about her years at UND and the honor she felt in calling herself a Sioux Alumni.

Then my husband spoke about a timeline from 2007 until today. He told them of how the State Board and the Chancellor worked against us and how UND staff aided the opposition before the vote on Spirit Lake. He gave specifics on dates and events. He also pointed out the Minot newspaper story on President Douple.

He was followed by Linus End of Horn who told about being home on leave, from the Army in 1969, and how he drove the official delegation from Standing Rock to Grand Forks for the Ceremony.

We ended up with Sean Johnson and his experiences at UND and just how meaningful the name and logo were to him as well as the majority of alumni. It was after 1 PM and we had been up for almost 3 hours by then. It was suggested, we adjourn for lunch and resume at 2 PM. The Chair said we will go until everyone had their chance and that after lunch the neutrals would be up. Haha...neutrals!!

There was not enough time for us to go out and eat, so we went to the cafeteria in the Capital Building and had a bite. We talked about the morning events and expressed our feelings on how it went. We were feeling pretty upbeat.

As we took our seats in the conference room the so-called "neutrals" were getting ready for their presentation and first up was Grant Shaft head of the State Board committee on the name and logo since February 2009.

Mr. Shaft started off with "Although I am neutral and have no position on the issue; I'd like to address a few issues from this morning's testimony before I give my prepared remakes. First off it was said we aided the opposition. That never happened, never, no one ever did. We have always worked to find support.

In his prepared statement he again said that they had worked with supporters and he went on to say that they had worked with the Spirit Lake tribe to get the September 2009 resolution done and the wording of that resolution. All of which is false, the State Board committee may have worked with the Spirit Lake Chairwoman Myra Pearson, who was and is opposed to the name and logo, but they rejected all attempts by us supporters to work with them and had nothing to do with the final resolution.

My husband was so mad because in short, Mr. Shaft basically called him a liar about the attempts by UND staff to influence tribal members to reject the name and logo. Luckily, he had a copy of the Devils Lake Journal from April 17th, 2009 in which Professor Amy Philips was interviewed saying how harmful the name and logo are. He showed the whole newspaper to Grand Forks Herald reporter Chuck Haga, who's only comment, was "so what!"

Chairwoman Ms. Kelch questioned Mr. Shaft as to why they would allow an outside organization to dictate to our sovereign State as to what we must do. Who are they to tell North Dakota what it can and can't do? Mr. Shaft fails to mention what is clear at the bottom of his prepared statement; Requirements of NCAA (A namesake tribe approval) which UND has always had.

Basically the only responses from Mr. Shaft are related to the Settlement/Agreement and the NCAA is a private institution. Also that he and the State Board tried to work to get approval from the tribes and worked with Spirit Lake in helping write the resolution of September 2009. *Again, these are false statements; they had nothing to do with the "Perpetual Resolution".*

After Mr. Shaft was finished came President Kelley (President of UND) although he claimed to be neutral on the name and logo, he had concerns about the Big Sky and whether they would accept UND if we keep the name and logo and how important it was to join the Big Sky.

123

He talked about the turmoil over the name, and was asked by a few of the legislators, who had graduated from UND just when and where this turmoil has been taking place. Because, in their years at UND they never saw it. He also denied the allegations by President Douple about being pressured. He added "To keep the name and logo could jeopardize the universities future". He also complained it would require them to break an agreement they had made with the NCAA. He was also asked about the cost of removing the logos at the arena and all over the university. His response was it has never been looked into and he had no idea of what the cost would be? Reason I mention this is just a few months earlier he stated "it would be more than $750,000".

Jon Backes (President of the State Board of Higher Ed.) was up next and spoke about all the other universities that had to change or suffer the consequences. He said the NCAA sanctions should not be taken lightly and recommended retiring the name. He also came out in defense of President Kelley.

Followed by athletic Director Brian Fasion, who stressed the importance of moving up to division I, athletics? He felt that the name and logo would jeopardize the move. He also defended President Kelley saying he was at the meeting where President Douple claimed pressure was put on him to come out against the name and logo. He said no such pressure was ever applied.

The common theme from all was that they were neutral and had no opinion on whether to pass a law or not. They were just presenting the facts. For having no opinion they did a better job than the opponents who were up next, but their "so-called" facts were not accurate, very misleading and in some cases absolutely not true.

But the committee decided to take a short break and adjourned for a half hour. We talked it over and decided we would leave for home after a quick bite to eat. While eating, we thought about it and Lavonne, Dave and I decided we would stay to hear the opposition speak. We got a room at the Kelly Inn and returned to the Capital.

Because we were late in getting back we had missed Leigh Jeanotte and Erich Longie's presentations but were told that Erich really ran down our tribal members and how uneducated they are. Both

124

had talked about the supposedly hostile environment at UND, but could provide no proof of what they claimed.

But we walked in while Jesse Taken Alive was getting up to speak. He started by talking in Sioux for about 2 minutes. I'm sure that most people did not understand a word he said, myself for one. I'm sure many were wondering just what he was saying about them, but then he began to speak in English.

He spoke the words that come out of many socialist mouths, he talked about de-colonization and ethnic genocide; he talked about a murder in Grand Forks but failed to mention it was committed by Native on Native and had nothing to do with the name or logo. He talked about a fight at UND but failed to mention it was over a love triangle and had nothing to do with the name or logo. He spoke about all the resolutions from Standing Rock but failed to mention that tribal members kept demanding to have their say, on the issue.

Next was Professor Birgit Hans, a recently naturalize German immigrant and head of the Native American Studies at UND. She told of how she could not conduct her classes properly because this issue always created so much turmoil in her classes. That the name must go, to stop the turmoil in the classroom.

A young lady who I believe she said was from a tribe in Washington State, but is living on the Cheyenne River reservation accused the citizens of Grand Forks of driving around with shot guns pointed out the window looking for Indians. When asked if she ever reported it, she said "no because the authorities wouldn't do anything about it anyway."

I believe it was after 8 PM when the hearing ended and the house Education Committee did not make their recommendations until February 16th, 2011. The House bill no. 1263 was sent to the ND Senate Education Committee, with the recommendation of "Do Pass" which the House Education Committee passed by a vote of 10 in favor and 5 opposing.

HOUSE BILL NO. 1263
    University of North Dakota fighting Sioux nickname and logo

    The Intercollegiate Athletic teams sponsored by the University of North Dakota shall be known as the University of North Dakota Fighting Sioux. Neither the University of North Dakota nor State Board of Higher Education may take any action to discontinue the use of the Fighting Sioux nickname or the Fighting Sioux logo in use on January 1, 2011. Any actions taken by the State Board of Higher Education and the University of North Dakota before the effective date of this Act to discontinue the use of the Fighting Sioux nickname and logo are preempted by this Act. If the National Collegiate Athletic Association takes any action to penalize the University of North Dakota for using the Fighting Sioux nickname or logo, the Attorney General shall consider filing a Federal Antitrust claim against that Association.

CHAPTER 13: THE NEXT HURDLE

After the House Education Committee voted, we were feeling good about our presentation to the Education Committee and its recommendation. We still had to wait to see what the full house would do. It wasn't until February 21st, 2011 and it was just what we had hoped for. The anxious moments and days we had been going through since the committee vote, were now at an end, but the battle was far from over.

We now went about preparing for the next step, the Senate Education Committee hearing to be held on March 7th, 2011. We were told it will be harder to convince them than it was with the House, but again we have come too far to turn back now and we have truth on our side.

My son who is a Benson County Commissioner suggested we try to talk to Senator Heckaman who represents Spirit Lake's district and is on the State Education Committee. We contacted her and set-up a meeting at the Old Main restaurant in Devils Lake. It was late February or early March of 2011 when we met.

I had called John Chaske after talking with Ms. Heckaman and he assured me he would be at the meeting. Ms. Heckaman arrived about 5:30 PM and we all introduced ourselves and shook hands. Ms. Heckaman as a Democrat had concerns due to the fact that the bill's sponsor was Al Carlson a Republican and a graduate of NDSU Bison, "why would he sponsor such a bill?" she wondered if he was trying to damage UND, that right now she opposes the bill.

We shared just how we felt Mr. Carlson was sincere in his efforts, but even if he were not keeping the name and logo was our goal and in the worst case scenario NCAA sanctions would only have minor impact on UND. We told her of the deceit and distortions that have and are still put out by the ND State board as well as the UND President Robert Kelly Administration.

She also brought up the subject of how the Democratic party works so closely with Native Americans and how they had endorsed Erich Longie for the North Dakota House of Representatives. We then reminded her that Erich was soundly defeated and barely got his own family to vote for him and that was because he opposed the vast majority of tribal members who had voted 67% in support of the name and logo. It is that big of an issue to tribal members and we asked, would she support her constituents on the reservation? We told her about the 1969 Sacred Ceremony and how once a name has been given and the Pipe smoked it cannot be undone by anyone. We asked her to press Jesse Taken Alive on the importance of our Sacred Ceremonies when the Senate hearings take place. By the end of our meeting, she said if we can back up what we had told her she would have to consider voting in favor of the bill. We assured her that everything we had said could be backed up by the facts. We thanked her for taking the time to meet with us and also for listening.

For the next couple of weeks we contacted tribal members asking if they could make the trip to Bismarck for the hearing.

Again we traveled to Bismarck the night before and again we met in the evening to talk about what might happen tomorrow. We had a newcomer Bill LeCaine who was one of the first Sioux warriors to actually play for UND hockey in the 50's and went on to play in the NHL for 11 years. Gaylord Peltier a tribal member of Turtle Mountain Chippewa was another who came to support us on the name and logo.

David brought his full box of binders and looked pretty comical carrying them around, I felt a little bit sorry for him because no one else paid attention to any of the information he had collected "It does become very useful in the days to come."

OUR COMMITTEE AND SUPPORTERS.

But here we go; again we were up first after the legislators, who wanted to speak (normal procedures). It started at 8 AM and was to go until noon, but again it was extended.

John was up first and repeated much of what he said at the House Hearing, he emphasized educational opportunities the name and logo bring to our people, the disrespect for our Circle of Medicine, and how we have fought the ND State Board of Higher Education.

Diane Gates spoke about her father Edward Loon who was a prominent member of the Standing Rock Government and his role in the 1969 Ceremony at UND.

I came next and reiterated my House testimony and just how the name and logo had help restore my self-esteem.

Archie followed and told of how their Tribal Council lacked the authority to reject and dismiss the 1969 Ceremony. That under their Constitution a petition signed by 20% of tribal members required a tribal vote to be held and just how the Council kept tabling the issue.

Gaylord Peltier, a UND graduate and member of the Turtle Mountain Tribe of Chippewa was next and spoke about his experiences at UND and his support for the name and logo. He also spoke about his son who attended UND and was elected President of UNDIA (the University of North Dakota Indian Association) but had to resign because of the uncomfortable feelings he had to endure because of he came out publically in support for the name and logo.

Spirit Lake Tribal member Renita DeLorme spoke of her time at the University and the help she received from her fellow white students at UND. She also spoke about the lack of assistance from the Native American Center on campus, although she did not know the reason for it, she stopped going there. She also expressed her anger over the head of UNDʼs Native American Centers statement that we members of Spirit Lake were not level headed because we didnʼt agree with him.

Then a young Spirit Lake Tribal member and student who was 16 years old expressed her hopes of attending UND and the name and logo made her proud to be a Sioux.

She was followed by Earl Strinden and Gordon Caldis both UND graduates, Earl talked about the 80 years of traditions and respect that UND had exhibited and Gordon talked about the NCAAʼs policy and just how there is NO Policy that has been adopted by the NCAA Constitutional Convention as Requirements.

Then came one of our new friends, Bill LeCaine, who is a Lakota Sioux born in Canada and he was one, if not the first actual Sioux to play hockey for UND. His story is one of the most inspirational stories of success you will ever hear. In the 1950ʼs he rose out of poverty in Canada to become a successful businessman. Although, the name and logo was not the only thing that inspired him to attend UND, it did play a large part. After playing hockey at UND he went on to play pro hockey for the Pittsburgh Penguins. He spoke of how important the name and logo are to Native Americans.

Jody was up next and again spoke about the "so-called" sanctions and just how important or *"unimportant"* they really are and he was followed by Kris Casement, a former UND graduate and member of the Fighting Sioux club.

JOHN CHASKE

DIANNE GATES

ARCHIE FOOL BEAR

EUNICE DAVIDSON

GAYLORD PELTIER

RENITA DeLORME

EARL STRINDEN

GORDON CALDIS

BILL LeCAINE

JODY HODGSON

LINUS END OF HORN

COMMITTE
MEMBERS
TESTIFYING
IN BISMARCK.

Linus End of horn was our final presenter of what turned out to be our morning session. He expressed that after receiving a BA degree at the University of South Dakota he transferred to UND Fighting Sioux because as a coyote from the University of South Dakota he was tired of being eaten by the Sioux. He also told of having been in a few bar

fights over the name, but said it was just drunk stupidity and if you can't stand the heat get out of the kitchen.

It was at this point our allotted time had run out and the opposition was up now, we had used up our 1 and half hours.

The opposition started off with Jesse Taken Alive who again spoke for a few minutes in Lakota as if that should make him something special. To me, it was a sign of disrespect to enter someone's home and intentionally speak in a dialect you know they don't understand.

He had a helper hand out a stack of papers to each committee member; each stack was over 2 inches thick and was the same as those handed out at the House Hearing. It was all the same stuff signed by the same people, which amounted to about 5 individuals. He then proceeded to threaten the legislators that if they pass this law he would unite all the South Dakota Tribal Governments in protest. He spoke of the many incidents that were supposedly had to occur at UND and Grand Forks. Again, there was not one bit of evidence to back up these allegations. He said there is no evidence to prove the 1969 Ceremony even happened.

When asked by Senator Heckaman as to whether or not the Tribal Council has the power to overturn Tribal Sacred Ceremonies, he did a great job of dancing around the question by saying "does the Protestant religion trump the Catholic religion?" but never really answered her question. Jesse always left me thinking (huh?).

When asked by Senator Gary Lee why the tribal members were not given the opportunity to have their petition honored with a tribal wide vote, he answered "another attorney said we were right and well within our realm to act the way we did".

Mr. Backes President of the ND State board testified that they were leaving behind their neutral position and now opposes the bill because

132

of the Settlement signed with the NCAA in 2007. He states that the NCAA Executive Committee was working to take charge of Native American imagery when the settlement was signed. He also states that the ND State board believed they'd be able to get support from the two tribes but that didn't happen. In 2006, the ND State board believed the NCAA Executive Committee did not have the authority to adopt the policy but things have changed. He also suggested the sanctions could be more severe than what is currently proposed. To pass this bill will be a death penalty for UND athletics.

Grant Shaft also of the ND State board basically said the same. He added that he disagrees with Representative Carlson and Representative Dosch: "They are misinformed and did not want to get the information to present to the full House ".

Chase Iron Eyes, an assistant in house attorney for the Standing Rock Tribe followed by saying; "You can vote a DO PASS to please your constituents and let the Governor deal with it. It's a tough choice, but it's the nature of a Republican form of Government. He added that there were two petitions circulated on Standing Rock; one for and one against a vote by the members".

My opinion, "Now I don't know about you, but for me, it sounds stupid to do a petition to stop a petition. I also don't know if it is legal to silence the voice of those you disagree with. The last Tribal Chairman election had a total of 1,928 votes cast and any petition to require a vote needs 20% of the total votes cast in the last election, the "1,004" individuals that signed the petition represent 52% from the last election and should have had a Constitutional right to a voice". (Bismarck Tribune)

It was time to break for noon lunch so we adjourned till the afternoon and would resume with more of the opposition after lunch. But because of the amount of testimony we would finish the day with testimony from the supporters later in the afternoon session.

Brian Faison Athletic Director at UND was up next and followed the ND State Board; lead, by presenting information that was consistent with their testimony. He talked about how UND will compete in Division I, starting in 2012 and all 20 athletic programs could be threatened. He stated that the women's hockey team is getting better and should be in the top 4 making them eligible for home field in playoff games, but that would not happen if we keep the name. We may not even be able to join any leagues with this name. He spoke of Minnesota and in the future of how they will not schedule any games with UND as long as they have the name and logo. It will end the scheduling of games with Wisconsin also.

Again he failed to mention that both Minnesota and Wisconsin are joining the Big 10 and UND is joining the NCHC (National Collegiate Hockey Conference) and no games will be scheduled anyway. That the only time Minnesota or Wisconsin would ever meet UND it would be in NCAA playoff games and to refuse to play UND at those times would mean they would be forfeiting the game.

Then there were some students from UND who talked about how because of the name UND was denied participation in a number of athletic events. The students were Tyler Rose, Grant Hauschild, Robert Boyd, and Margret Scott. (Source: Minutes from the Senate Education Committee Hearing)

At this time because the opposition had much more time to present their case, their time was cut off leaving the rest to submit written remarks and the Chair called for anymore in support to step to the podium. As my husband stepped up to the podium, he was cut off by Leigh Jeanotte, head of the Native American Center, in an attempt to speak in opposition. The chair had to interrupt him saying the time left is for supporters.

My husband who had thought he would not have time to testify, realized, he would be given an opportunity, so during the noon break, he rushed back to the room to get his testimony ready. When the floor switched back to the supporters he was ready and eager to correct some of the testimony given in opposition. He finally got his chance to respond to being called a liar at the House hearing by Grant Shaft. He supplied the DVD of Amy Philips in April 16, 2009 and a copy of the Devils Lake Journal where she is trying to influence the upcoming vote on the name and logo at Spirit Lake in April 2009. Along with his statement to the effect the ND State board never attempted to get any support for the name and logo, he submitted a packet of facts to back up everything he said. His anger to the distorted and misleading

LEFT: My Husband David RIGHT: Lavonne Alberts

information presented by the opposition clearly showed on his face as he spoke.

He was followed by Committee member Lavonne Alberts who spoke to the respect or the lack of respect that has happened over the years. Lavonne spoke out about how we have a Tribal Chair who did not support the issue, but Spirit Lake was allowed a vote! She re-iterated the fact that 67% of the enrolled members of Spirit Lake voiced their support along with the resolution from 2009.

Then came Sean Johnson, alumni of UND giving the history as he knew it at his time at UND. He was followed by Senator Hogue urging support for the bill, and he also added an amendment that might gather support for the bill.

This ended the hearing and we had to wait for their recommendation to the full North Dakota Senate. We were not surprised but disappointed with the recommendation to the Senate. It left the committee two days later with a "do not pass", but it did have the amendment in it. The vote was 2 in favor and 5 opposed. Our Spirit Lake representative Senator Heckaman, decided to vote against her constituents, which very much surprised me due to the 67% vote that was given by the largest voting bloc in her District. I thought what kind of person does that??

135

On March 11th, 2011, the full Senate voted 28 to 15 in favor of the new law. We had been able to watch the vote as it happened on our computers and even there we were disheartened because the first votes to be registered were opposed to the bill, but then it happened and the vote tally turned in our favor. We cheered out loud as we saw the final vote tally, only one more hurdle.   The Governor said he would sign it into law. On March 17th, 2011 it became law after the Governor signed the bill with an amendment.

An amendment was added to the bill that no more than a million dollars of state money could be spent on any legal action that might come from the bill. The whole transcript of the House and Senate hearings are in PDF form. Google: (2011 House Education HB 1263, 13509).

We had finally won, our battle was over, or so we thought. The satisfaction and peace of mind was only to last a few months.

The opposition seamed to go into full attack mode and back door tactics. It did not take long for a meeting with the NCAA to be set. This is something we expected to see if any further legal steps were going to be necessary or if they could be avoided.

CHAPTER 14: IT NEVER STOPS

After the Governor signed the bill into law on March 17th, again, we thought we were finally able to relax, but as usual we could not relax for long, because of the small groups that we consider them as hypocrites.

The Grand Forks Herald had been printing a number of stories about the law being un-constitutional, also how damaging the name and image was to the University. They implied we would be denied acceptance in any division 1 athletic conference.

A meeting with the NCAA was set up for April 22, 2011 to be held in Bismarck. We felt confident that the NCAA Executive Committee would recognize the determination and resolve that had carried this battle to the extent of passing a State law, all because of the determination of the actual Sioux people.

We felt Federal law, the NCAA Constitution by-laws, NCAA exemption requirements, the determination and resolve we have shown, and the voices of Sioux people of North Dakota as well as our 1969 ceremony were all on our side, so how could they just ignore us with all of this in our favor, but that is just what happened!

It started by letters to the editor from the opposition that found no resistance in getting them printed. Anyone who disagreed with the opposition stance was hinted as being a racist and promoting racism or the destruction of the University. The same old pattern we had been dealing with for the last 4 years of distorted stories with no proof to back them up were printed almost daily.

But now the State law said we were right and should have been a buffer too these minority groups of agitators and anarchists. There was also the stories of the Big Sky and how the name and image may prevent UND"s admission. Doug Fullerton President of the Big Sky had made many statements that UND"s name and image may cause problems for the league. It appears that Mr. Fullerton's comments were requested by the UND Administration.

As for the scheduled meeting with the NCAA on April 22, 2011 we at Spirit Lake had expressed our desire to be included. Archie and his group on Standing Rock had expressed their desire to be included also. One way or another we were going to be in Bismarck for the meeting whether or not we were allowed a voice at the meeting.

After talking to some of the state politicians about our desire to have a voice at the NCAA and UND meeting, we were advised that it may not be possible. We asked "Who could be more important than the Sioux themselves? Why would we be left out again?"

As the day for the meeting approached a familiar pattern reared its ugly head again. On April 15th AP news reports flashed "The NCAA would not be coming to attend the meeting" and it was cancelled.

In responding to e-mails from President Kelley, Bernard Franklin (NCAA Vice President) and Mark Emmett (President of NCAA) in an email message back to Robert Kelley (President of The University of North Dakota) on Wednesday April 15th, 2011, said the "Difference of opinion seems to transcend the nickname/logo issue to the fundamental matters of governmental operation and authority." The NCAA, Franklin wrote, "Has no role in that discussion" and because it probably would be open to the public, the NCAA declined to attend. (Associated Press)

Dalrymple, Stenehjem, Kelley, Shaft and the North Dakota Legislature's GOP majority leaders, Bismarck Senator Bob Stenehjem and Fargo Rep. Al Carlson, had been invited to attend the meeting, along with UND's athletics director, Brian Faison; William Goetz, the chancellor of the state university system; and Jon Backes, president of the Board of Higher Education.

The meeting was to be closed to the public, which prompted protests from The Associated Press and other media organizations, and the Legislature's Democratic leaders. Dalrymple, who is a Republican, told the AP he believed the meeting should be open.

Bernard Franklin's email declaring that NCAA officials would not attend came days after Kelley, in his own email to Franklin, mentioned the objections and said that "members of the public may be in attendance, as will state and local media."

Shaft said Emmert and Franklin had committed to come to Bismarck for the meeting. The only circumstance that changed was information in Kelley's email that the meeting might be open to the public. We could not get access to President Kelley's e-mail and can only wonder just what he said.

But because of his past actions and President Douple's statement, we could only wonder just what was in Kelley's e-mail, we had heard that Kelley had solicited most of President Fullerton's comments and things just smelt fishy to us.

But this was something that caught us off guard for it was Bernard Franklin himself that said on October 27th, 2007 that "The Sioux people and NO ONE ELSE should decide if and how the name and logo should be used", now he does not want our voice heard! As far as I'm concerned, he is nothing more than a hypocrite. This was not a meeting about the State Government and the NCAA was only going to be there to decide if exemption was fitting and proper as so many other Universities had already received with much less effort being exerted.

All the evidence needed had already been found and was just waiting for a court battle if necessary. The requirement that so many other Universities had received exemption from the NCAA Executive Committee Policy had been more than met here in North Dakota.

A million dollars had been pledged in the new Law to fight the NCAA if necessary. The NCAA which had been in a weak position in the 2007 lawsuit was now in an even weaker position, why would they wish to return to court?

But now there was going to be no meeting and the courts might have to be the next step, the new North Dakota Law said the State was to expend no more than a million dollars to pursue a legal challenge.

The State Legislators and Governor had just taken a stand with the Sioux people of North Dakota and the citizens were behind us. We as Sioux people had started off just doing what was asked of us, and then on to fighting the NCAA, UND, the Settlement/Agreement, on to the State Board of Higher Ed., to the UND Administration and Professors, and lobbyists, we face distortions, lies, character assassination, and ridicule, but had finally prevailed.   What could go wrong now?

There was much concern about just what President Kelley had conveyed to the NCAA. After President Douple of the Summit League and President Fullerton of the Big Sky Conference statements of e-mails and phone conversations as well as meetings, one can only wonder just what he was saying or if he was encouraging the NCAA to stand firm?

There were all kinds of statements and letters in the press; it seemed like a daily occurrence. Out of everything printed I don't recall even one story that was of a positive nature about the name and logo and our efforts. They were always about the Big Sky and how UND may not be accepted into it, leaving UND out in the cold.

Now for some truth: UND President Robert Kelley and Big Sky President Doug Fullerton both signed the contract for UND's admission into the Big Sky on October 26th of 2010, and we were known as the Fighting Sioux at that time. Montana papers reported the "Sioux Are Coming" after the contract signing, then the Big Sky football schedule through the year 2015 was announced on April 22nd of 2011 and UND Fighting Sioux were on it, and the State Law said for months now, we are to be known as the UND Fighting Sioux.

A breach of a legal contract would be the only way to remove UND and it would require all 12 other Big Sky Universities to agree to the removal and to date not one had suggested doing so. President Fullerton had no authority to remove UND and was just blowing hot air to help Chancellor Goetz and President Kelley and their group of agitators.

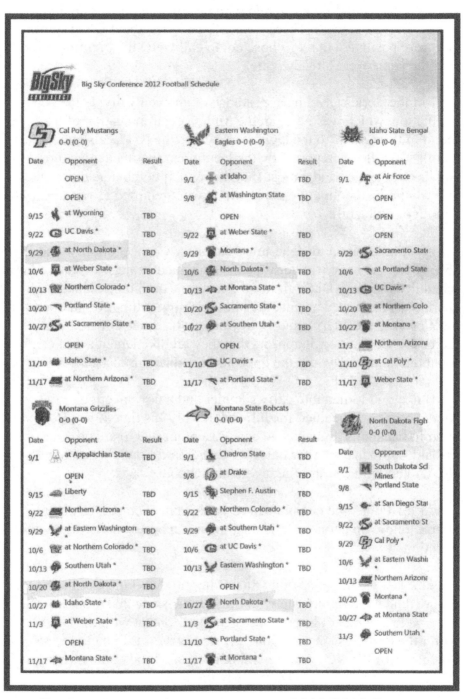

Big Sky Conference 2012 Football Schedule

Cal Poly Mustangs 0-0 (0-0)

Date	Opponent	Result
	OPEN	
	OPEN	
9/15	at Wyoming	TBD
9/22	UC Davis *	TBD
9/29	at North Dakota *	TBD
10/6	at Weber State *	TBD
10/13	Northern Colorado *	TBD
10/20	Portland State *	TBD
10/27	at Sacramento State *	TBD
	OPEN	
11/10	Idaho State *	TBD
11/17	at Northern Arizona *	TBD

Eastern Washington Eagles 0-0 (0-0)

Date	Opponent	Result
9/1	at Idaho	TBD
9/8	at Washington State	TBD
	OPEN	
9/22	at Weber State *	TBD
9/29	Montana *	TBD
10/6	North Dakota *	TBD
10/13	at Montana State *	TBD
10/20	Sacramento State *	TBD
10/27	at Southern Utah *	TBD
	OPEN	
11/10	UC Davis *	TBD
11/17	at Portland State *	TBD

Idaho State Bengals 0-0 (0-0)

Date	Opponent
9/1	at Air Force
	OPEN
	OPEN
	OPEN
9/29	Sacramento State
10/6	at Portland State
10/13	UC Davis *
10/20	at Northern Colo
10/27	at Montana *
11/3	Northern Arizona
11/10	at Cal Poly *
11/17	Weber State *

Montana Grizzlies 0-0 (0-0)

Date	Opponent	Result
9/1	at Appalachian State	TBD
	OPEN	
9/15	Liberty	TBD
9/22	Northern Arizona *	TBD
9/29	at Eastern Washington *	TBD
10/6	at Northern Colorado *	TBD
10/13	Southern Utah *	TBD
10/20	at North Dakota *	TBD
10/27	Idaho State *	TBD
11/3	at Weber State *	TBD
	OPEN	
11/17	Montana State *	TBD

Montana State Bobcats 0-0 (0-0)

Date	Opponent	Result
9/1	Chadron State	TBD
9/8	at Drake	TBD
9/15	Stephen F. Austin	TBD
9/22	Northern Colorado *	TBD
9/29	at Southern Utah *	TBD
10/6	at UC Davis *	TBD
10/13	Eastern Washington *	TBD
	OPEN	
10/27	North Dakota *	TBD
11/3	at Sacramento State *	TBD
11/10	Portland State *	TBD
11/17	at Montana *	TBD

North Dakota Figh 0-0 (0-0)

Date	Opponent
9/1	South Dakota Scl Mines
9/8	Portland State
9/15	at San Diego Star
9/22	at Sacramento St
9/29	Cal Poly *
10/6	at Eastern Washir *
10/13	Northern Arizona
10/20	Montana *
10/27	at Montana State
11/3	Southern Utah *
	OPEN

BIG SKY FOOTBALL SCHEDULE FOR THE 2012-2013 SEASON

Between March 17th and April 16th, 2011, (30 days) there were 41 stories in the Grand Forks Herald with negative overtones about the name and logo in them. There were a few stories about UND sports that were positive, but they chose not to call UND the Fighting Sioux as if the name were already gone.

But the stories gave the appearance of an evenly divided state population, which was far from the truth, a clear indication of it can be found in the e-mails to the legislators before the ND Legislators voted on bill 1263. It was reported by the local press that the legislature's emails over loaded and almost shut down their computers due to the overwhelming amount of emails, which were reported as running 19 to 1 in favor of the bill.

Looking back on the lead-up to the NCAA cancellation on April 15th, 2011, one must wonder was this a planned strategy to scuttle the scheduled meeting. Did it fit into Executive Committee plans? Democrats that voted against the bill were now calling for an open meeting with the NCAA and from what we have seen of the NCAA Executive Committee, it appears that they are like Dracula and can't stand the light of day; did the opposition realize this also?

But spring turned into early summer and a new meeting with the NCAA was re- scheduled for July 25th, 2011, this time it was going to be in Indianapolis, Indiana and again we requested to attend. Our Tribal Chairman sent a formal letter to Bernard Franklin and the NCAA committee requesting a seat at the table.

At least this time he did get a response, but even that came only after a follow-up phone call demanding a response, but it was another rejection.

The first paragraph is quite misleading in that it implies the NCAA was willing to communicate with Spirit Lake since 2007, but in fact, there were a number of times we attempted contact with the NCAA with little or no response. Again, as I said early, I truly believe these executives of the NCAA were sitting back laughing at the turmoil they caused out here in North Dakota. My thoughts.

SPIRIT LAKE TRIBE

PO Box 359 • Fort Totten, ND 58335 • Phone: 701-766-4221 • Fax 701-766-4126

Dr. Bernard Franklin
P.O. Box 6222
Indianapolis, IN 46206-6222

July 7, 2011

Dear Dr. Bernard Franklin and NCAA Sanctioning Committee,

A 'hua! (Greetings) from Spirit Lake Tribe North Dakota!

The purpose of this letter is to express to you our sincere desire to have representation of the Spirit Lake Tribe at the table during the discussion between the NCAA and the State of North Dakota concerning the use of our name- the Fighting Sioux - at the University of North Dakota. Although much has been written on the subject in the media, it is all distorted and biased. For decades, the general public listened to the media espouse the "official" position of Spirit Lake, only to see that position trounced in an actual election. As the elected leaders of this tribe we are writing to you on behalf of the 67% of the voting population of Spirit Lake Tribe and the Tribal Council that support the use of the Fighting Sioux by UND.

The NCAA has always presented and encouraged cultural diversity within its organization. As proud members of the Dakota Sioux Tribe which is the only Sioux Tribe within the boundaries of the State of North Dakota, we appreciate that effort and we request to be included and present during the scheduled discussion of the future of the Fighting Sioux name and logo.

Cordially,

Roger Yankton Sr.
Chairman.

Darwin Brown
Mission District Representative

LETTER FROM THE SPIRIT LAKE TRIBAL COUNCIL
(TEXT AS FOLLOWS)

Dr. Bernard Franklin
P.O. Box 6222
Indianapolis, IN 46206-6222
July 7, 2011

Dear Bernard Franklin and NCAA Sanctioning Committee.

A 'hua! (Greetings) from Spirit Lake North Dakota!

The purpose of this letter is to express to you our sincere desire to have representation of the Spirit Lake Tribe at the table during the discussion between the

NCAA and the State of North Dakota concerning the use of our name- the Fighting Sioux- at the University of North Dakota. Although much has been written on the subject in the media, it is all distorted and biased. For decades, the general public listened to the media espouse the "official" position of Spirit Lake, only to see that position trouced in an actual election. As the elected leaders of this tribe we are writing to you on behalf of the 67% of the voting population of Spirit Lake Tribe and the Tribal Copuncil that support the use of the Fighting Sioux by UND.

The NCAA has always presented and encouraged cultural diversity within its organization. As proud members of the Dakota Sioux Tribe which is the only Sioux Tribe within the boundaries of the State of North Dakota, we appreciate that effort and we request to be included and present during the scheduled discussion of the future of the Fighting Sioux name and logo.

Cordially

Roger Yankton

Sr.Chairman

DarwinBrown

Mission District Representative

July 20, 2011

'0. Box 6222
ndianapolis, Indiana 46206
Telephone: 317/917-6222

Shipping/Overnight Address:
802 Alonzo Watford Sr. Drive
ndianapolis, Indiana 46202

www.ncaa.org

Mr. Roger Yankton Sr.
Chairman
Spirit Lake Tribe
P.O. Box 359
Fort Totten, North Dakota 58335

Dear Mr. Yankton:

Thank you for recent your correspondence. I appreciate your willingness to keep the lines of communication open.

Regarding the upcoming meeting, I would encourage you to work closely with the university as well as your state representatives to ensure opportunities for discussion and inclusion. Given the terms of the settlement agreement between the University of North Dakota and the NCAA, as well as recent legislative action within the state, this appears to be the most appropriate avenue at this time.

Sincerely,

Bernard W. Franklin
Executive Vice President of Membership and Student-Athlete Affairs/
    Chief Inclusion Officer

BWF:jw

National Collegiate Athletic Association
An association of over 1,200 members serving the student-athlete
Equal Opportunity/Affirmative Action Employer

NCAA RESPONSE. (TEXT AS FOLLOWS)

July 20, 2011

Mr. Roger Yankton Sr.
Chairman
P.O. Box 359
Fort Totten, North Dakota 58335

Dear Mr. Yankton:

Thank you for recent correspondence. I appreciate your willingness to keep the lines of communication open.

Regarding the upcoming meeting, I would encourage you to work closely with the university as well as your state representatives to ensure opportunities for discussion and inclusion. Given the terms of the settlement agreement between the University of North Dakota and the NCAA, as well as recent Legislative action within the state, this appears to be the most appropriate avenue at this time.

Sincerely,

Bernard W. Franklin

Executive Vice President of Membership and Student Affairs/Chief Inclusion Officer

We feel there is a completely different reason behind this so-called policy and it has nothing in any way to do with what Native American Indians feel. The Executive Committee could care less what we think. That is why they don't want us at the table, is what I've come to believe.

Passing the buck seems to be a common theme with the NCAA, ND State board and Kelley Administration. It's always someone else's fault.

The NCAA says it's up to the University if they want the actual Sioux present and the University and ND State board says it's the NCAA that has cancelled because the actual Sioux will be there, but this is nothing new, for the last 4 years we Sioux have been used when convenient and discarded when inconvenient.

But a new meeting is set for July 25th, 2011 and the most important voice has been silenced, the attendees will be Representative Carlson (House majority leader), Senator Bob Stenehjem (Senate majority leader and brother to the State Attorney General) and Jody Hodgson (Ralph Engelstad Arena manager) in support of the Sioux people, the REA and the name and image.

Then there is Chancellor Goetz (Chancellor ND State board), Grant Shaft (ND State board President), Robert Kelley (President of UND), Brian Faison (Athletic Director at UND), and North Dakota Governor Dalrymple in opposition.

I'm sure they will say they weren't in opposition of the name and logo, but it is easy to say anything you like, but it's your actions that tell the truth. True, I wasn't at the meeting and can only guess at what actually transpired at the meeting when it finally did take place.

But it had to be postponed again because of a tragic event that took place days before the meeting; Senator Bob Stenehjem was killed in a tragic accident. He was going to be one of our strongest voices at the meeting. My heart was broken for Mr. Stenehjem's family, I never got to meet him personally, but he truly expressed his stance on this issue. I will always think of him as a "Warrior" and a man of honor.

The meeting finally took place on August 12, 2011 and opposition out weighted the supporters 5 to 1. In attendance at the meeting Representative Al Carlson who had sponsored bill HB 1263 and Jody Hodgson was representing the REA.

Our longtime supporter and friend Jody was there with a double duty. He had stood with us from our committee's inception in 2008, but he also had to (as general manager) represent the REA which would have to go on regardless of the outcome from the meeting with the NCAA. If they were not to give an exemption to UND, he had to try to minimize the damage to REA architecture. There were over 2400 logos throughout the building and the cost to remove them would be immense. He had to walk a thin line and try to work with supporters and the NCAA.

Some have said to me that Jody had turned on our committee, but I think to myself, Jody had to do what was best for the Ralph. It is his lively hood and I understood what he had to do. If it had been me, I can't say I wouldn't have done the same thing or I would have had to quit. To this day I still think of Jody as a good friend to us supporters, but he was caught in the middle.

Al Carlson, who had sponsored one of the three bills proposed to the Legislators and the one finally approved, was the only one there to speak for the Sioux of Spirit Lake and North Dakota Standing Rock members as well as citizens of North Dakota and 80 years of tradition.

So in truth there was only one voice that was there to push for truth, honor, and respect. I'm sure he felt quite lonely. I was not there

147

and can only give my opinions as to just what took place. From my viewpoint it is easy to reach the conclusion that Al was the lone voice in a sea of corruption.

It is not hard to believe that Chancellor Goetz through his statements was opposed to the Sioux from his appointment to Chancellor of the ND State board in July of 2007 and worked to dismantle 80 years of traditions from the beginning and would give encouragement to the NCAA Executive Committee.

It is not hard to believe that President Kelley was brought on board in July of 2008 to help with that destruction, when normal procedures were dispensed with so he was the only name submitted to the ND State board for consideration by Chancellor Goetz. I believe he brought his "Cal. State Berkeley" ideas with him. Not once have I ever heard him say he supported the name and logo or UND's 80 years of tradition, only that he was going to be neutral. That tells me a lot of where he stood.

I still don't understand why individuals from North Dakota were not good enough to take care of one of our own State taxpayer funded colleges. I think in order to keep up traditions of where you are from; you have to feel it in your soul.

It's not hard to believe that Grant Shaft who has been on record of openly opposing the continued use of the Fighting Sioux name and logo for some time now, would be less then forceful to the NCAA. I find it hard to believe he did anything but encourage the NCAA Executive Committee to hold firm.

It's not hard to believe Brian Faison another outsider brought in to be Athletic Director at UND was there to encourage opposition to the name and logo. He too was on record of opposing the continued use of the Fighting Sioux name & logo. For More Information on his comments and Frank Burggraf's response, see the article on page 214.

It is not hard to believe Governor Dalrymple who had just signed bill 1263 into law a few months ago was not fully supportive of the new law because of his wishy washy statements before the House and Senate voted on the new Law. It is easy to believe he only signed the Bill out of fear of the upcoming election in 2012. With the

148

overwhelming support for the law exhibited by his constituents, it would be a big gamble to go against them, but he can now say to supporters he tried his best, but my question is for what?

Immediately upon leaving the meeting with the NCAA Executive Committee in Indianapolis, the Governor went on record as to saying he was going to sponsor Legislation to repeal the law at the next special session beginning on November 7th, 2011. Is his true color showing?

There apparently was no consideration given to following through with the portion of State Law "1263" which required up to a million dollars to be spent on litigation, should it be necessary, leaving one to wonder, were we Sioux people used again. Were we just another bargaining chip, was this ever about respect? Why was the Governor not listening to the people of North Dakota? Was his statement, minutes after the meeting prepared in advance of the meeting? Did he know what the outcome of the meeting was to be? I have to ask myself these questions because to me it seems too obvious.

But here we were again, wondering, when is enough, enough, what do we have to do? Should we give up, roll over and play dead? Should we just accept, we are just Indians and have no meaning or value in the world of elite bigots? That we can be used by anyone at any time of convenience? Does truth have any value? Should we forsake our ancestors and go quietly in oblivion?

We are not so naïve as to think this is an earth shaking issue or that someone's life hangs in the balance, no one is going to die over the outcome (at least we hope not), but in truth it will affect every Native American to some degree. It will affect educational opportunities and self-esteem issues. It confirms the belief held by many Indians, that we are nothing in the eyes of the elite.

But the law is the law and until the law is repealed, UND is to stay the "Fighting Sioux", regardless of those "out of state as well as those in state agitators" and their bigoted position. I know I am painting the opposition with a broad brush, but I believe that the majority of the opposition lack moral or ethical values. Yet, I feel there are a few within the group, that for misguided reasons feel our names and images must be removed.

149

Over the next few months we pondered the question of what to do next. We started off being disillusioned and hurt, too darn angry, but still we weren't sure of just what to do or if anything could even be done. We had a few lawyers that have been standing with us and we turned to them for advice as to what options are left.

Reed Soderstrom, an attorney out of Minot had been representing Archie Fool Bear at Standing Rock for a couple of years now. He joined our cause and had testified at the House and Senate Education Committees with us.

Stephen Behm, an attorney out of Mankato, Minnesota had joined us at the Committee hearings also.

Gordon Caldis, a retired attorney out of Grand Forks who had been fighting this fight for more than 10 years and had written numerous articles as well as books on the subject, joined us in any way he could, the reference page in the back of the book dealing with the NCAA Manual and Constitution is dedicated to him and will show the NCAA Constitution, the NCAA Executive Committee, and By-Laws and just how we feel the (thanks to Gordon) NCAA Executive Committee has overstepped their Constitutional authority intentionally.

After the Education Committee hearings we had kept in contact with our new friends and attorneys. As our joy and satisfaction from the new State Law faded we had many discussions on new strategies and new challenges we may have to face.

To this point all our efforts had been focused within the State towards the North Dakota State Board of Higher Education, University of North Dakota Administration and Athletic conferences. We have relied on truth and justice but were countered with lies and distortions also the NCAA sanctions. If we are to go on, we must change our focus and challenge the NCAA itself. Could we, and if we could, how would we? At the North Dakota Supreme Court one of the concerns was our committee's legitimacy. We would need to address that issue. Damages would also have to be addressed.

But we had to do first things first and we had talks with Tribal officials in day to day conversations and they were aware and supportive of our efforts but nothing had been done as far as recognizing us as any kind of authoritative committee. It was understood we were un-officially representing Tribal member's views and had no actual authority to speak for the tribe.

We realized we needed some sort of official recognition and authorization to speak on behalf of the tribe. We also realized we could not be some ad hock group allowed to go wild on our own whims; we had to answer to someone and that being the Tribal Government.

A resolution from the Tribal Government was needed and John Chaske went to work on drawing one up to propose to the Tribal Council. On September 2nd, 2011, the Tribal Council met and revised the proposal wording and voted on it.

Now we are a recognized tribal entity with limited powers, but still a voice that has legitimacy. Our voice cannot be ignored or dismissed as a group of no-bodies or as was referred to as a (ADD HOCK GROUP). The opposition on Spirit Lake recognized that also and was hard at work trying to un-do what had been done.

As usual they believed the only voices to count were the opposition voices and to hell with the majority. Erich appeared to be working on anything that could help his cause. He seemed to be following what had been referred to by (Courtesy of Tu-Yuen-Tran of the Grand Forks Herald City Beat) back in 2009 as "The end justifies the means". Erich started another of his many petition drives against the Tribal Council and their resolution on September 2nd, 2011 (resolution # A05-11-174) and as usual he is unable to get enough support. The many petitions he started, all fall by the wayside, but it does not stop the Herald from printing stories about them. They make good headlines, but they never report that the petitions go nowhere.

But now we had direction again and were instructed to do whatever it takes to save the name and logo. A lawsuit against the NCAA was now our focus but before filing it, it would have to be cleared by the by the Tribal Government, as I said we had limited power and anything involving the tribe as a whole would have to be run by the Tribal Government and their attorney first.

SPIRIT LAKE SIOUX TRIBE
RESOLUTION NO. A05-11-174

WHEREAS, the Spirit Lake Tribe of Indians is a federally recognized American Indian tribe governed by a revised Constitution dated May 5, 1960, approved by Acting Commissioner, Bureau of Indian Affairs, July 14, 1961, and subsequently amended July 17, 1969; May 3, 1974; April 16, 1976; May 4, 1981; and August 19, 1996; and approved by the Commissioner, Bureau of Indian Affairs;

WHEREAS, the Constitution of the Spirit Lake Tribe generally authorizes and Empowers the Spirit Lake Tribal Council to engage in activities on behalf of and in the interest of the health and welfare and benefit of the Tribe and of the enrolled members thereof; and

WHEREAS, the Tribal Council, by and through Resolution No. A05-09-191, and pursuant to the vote of the people who chose the Tribal Council Representatives, affirmatively approved and supported UND's use of the name and imagery of the Fighting Sioux, and by overwhelming support of the people of this Tribe, entrusted UND with the responsibility of working with this Tribe to increase the number of Native American graduates from Spirit Lake and create a Native American program on the UND campus which would bring respect and understanding amongst all students, faculty and staff at UND; and

WHEREAS, the Tribal Council firmly abides by its Traditional Dakota Ceremonials and highly respects the Dakota Chiefs who gave their word ceremoniously with the sacred pipe and thereby consented to the 1867 Treaty with the U.S. Government, rendering this ceremonial act irreversible in accordance with Dakota Tradition; and

WHEREAS, without this Tribe's authorization, consent and without discussion, it is understood that the National Collegiate Athletic Association (NCAA), the North Dakota State Board of Higher Education, and others have issued sanctions, made plans to retire the honorable name Fighting Sioux, and have commenced lawsuits for enforcement;

WHEREAS, the Spirit Lake Tribal Council recognizes and approves the actions of the Spirit Lake Committee for Understanding and Respect, who were very instrumental in the initiation of the 2009 Tribal Referendum to keep the Fighting Sioux name at UND and who have provided testimony on Spirit Lake's behalf at the North Dakota state legislature successfully achieving the adoption of (HB#1263), making it unlawful to retire the Sioux name at UND.

NOW THEREFORE BE IT RESOLVED, the Tribal Council hereby authorizes the Committee for Understanding and Respect to act on behalf of the Spirit Lake Tribe to seek outside resources and support to defend Spirit Lake's Voice and

Page One: Spirit Lake Resolution

CONTINUED ON NEXT PAGE

Resolution No. A05-11-174
Page 2 of 2

UND's right to retain the Fighting Sioux Name. The authorized Membership consists of the following Spirit Lake Enrolled Members: Eunice Davidson, Renita DeLorme, LaVonne Alberts, Alex Yankton, Joseph Lawrence, Sr., John D. Chaske, Sr., and Frank Black Cloud. The Spirit Lake Tribal Council authorizes and appoints the following lawyers as well as their agents and assigns, the right to defend Resolution A05-09-191 so that the University of North Dakota shall remain known as the Fighting Sioux: Jerry Rice, Stephen Behm, and Reed Soderstrom. This authorization and appointment is conditioned that no tribal funds shall be utilized for payment of attorney fees or any other expenses incurred. This authorization and appointment includes said attorneys to proceed or intervene in any tribal, state or federal court on behalf of the Spirit Lake Sioux Tribe as a named party in any manner they deem appropriate so that UND shall remain known as the Fighting Sioux.

BE IT FURTHER RESOLVED, that this authorization and appointment includes going forward on a statewide initiated measure on behalf of the Spirit Lake Tribe.

CERTIFICATION

We, the undersigned, Chairman and Secretary of the Tribal Council do hereby certify that the Tribal Council is composed of six (6) members of whom five (5) were present, constituting a quorum, for a meeting duly and regularly called, noticed, convened and held on the 2nd day of SEPTEMBER, 2011, and approved this resolution by the affirmative vote of four (4) in favor, none (0) opposing, none (0) abstaining and none (0) absent. (The Secretary-Treasurer does not vote and the Chairman votes only in case of a tie)

Susie Fox
Recording Secretary

Roger Yankton Sr.
Chairman

PAGE TWO: SPIRIT LAKE RESOLUTION

RESOLUTION TEXT AS FOLLOWS:

Spirit Lake Sioux Tribe
Resolution No. A05-11-174

Whereas, the Spirit Lake Tribe of Indians is a federally recognized American Indian tribe governed by a revised Constitution dated May 5, 1960, approved by Acting Commissioner, Bureau of Indian Affairs, July 14, 1961, and subsequently amended July 17, 1969: May 3, 1974: April 16, 1976: May 4, 1981; and August 19, 1996 and approved by the Commissioner, Bureau of Indian Affairs;

Whereas, the Constitution of the Spirit Lake Tribe generally authorizes and empowers the Spirit Lake Tribal Council to engage in activities on behalf of and in the interest of the health and welfare and benefit of the Tribe and of the enrolled members thereof; and

***Whereas;** the Tribal Council, by and through Resolution No. A05-09-191, and pursuant to the vote of the people who chose the Tribal Council Representatives, affirmatively approved and supported UND's use of the name and imagery of the Fighting Sioux, and by overwhelming support of the people of the Tribe, enthused UND with the responsibility of working with this Tribe to increase the number of Native American graduates from Spirit Lake and create a Native American program on the UND campus which would bring respect and understanding amongst all students, faculty and staff at UND; and*

***Whereas;** the Tribal Council firmly abides by its Traditional Dakota Ceremonials and highly respects the Dakota Chiefs who gave their word ceremoniously with the sacred pipe and thereby consenting to the 1867 Treaty with the U.S. Government, rending this ceremonial act irreversible in accordance with Dakota Tradition; and*

***Whereas;** without this Tribe's authorization, consent and without discussion, it is understood that the National Collegiate Athletic Association (NCAA), the North Dakota State Board of Higher Education, and others have issued sanctions, made plans to retire the honorable name Fighting Sioux, and have commenced lawsuits for enforcement;*

***Whereas;** the Spirit Laske Tribal Council recognizes and approves the actions of the Spirit Lake Committee for Understanding and Respect, who were very instrumental in the initiation of the 2009 Tribal Referendum to keep the Fighting Sioux name at UND and who have provided testimony on behalf at the North Dakota state Legislature successfully achieving the adoption of (HB#1263), making it unlawful to retire the Sioux name at UND*

***Now Therefore Be It Resolved**, the Tribal Council hereby authorizes the Committee for Understanding and Respect to act on behalf of the Spirit Lake Tribe to seek outside resources and support to defend Spirit Lake's and (page 2) UND's right to retain the Fighting Sioux Name. The authorized Membership consists of the following Spirit Lake Enrolled Members; Eunice Davidson, Renita DeLorme, LaVonne Alberts, Alex Yankton, Joseph Lawrence, Sr., John Chaske, Sr., and Frank Black Cloud. The Spirit Lake Tribal Council authorizes and appoints the following lawyers as well as their agents and assigns, the right to defend Resolution A05-09-191 so that the University of North Dakota shall remain known as the Figthing Sioux; Jerry Rice, Stephen Behm, Reed Soderstrom. This authorization and appointment is conditioned that no tribal funds shall be utilized for payment of attorney fees or any other expenses incurred. This authorization and appointment includes said attorneys to proceed or intervene in any tribal, state, or federal court on behalf of the Spirit Lake Tribe as a named party in any manner they deem appropriate so that UND shall remain known as the Fighting Sioux.*

***Be It Further Resolved**, that this authorization and appointment includes going forward on a statewide initiated measure on behalf of the Spirit Lake Tribe.*

CERTIFICATION

We, the undersigned, Chairman and Secretary of the Tribal Council do hereby certify that the Tribal Council is composed of six (6) members of whom five (5) were present, constituting a quorum , for a meeting and regularly called, noticed, convened and held on the 2nd, day of SEPTEMBER, 2011, and approved this resolution by the affirmative vote of Four (4) in favor, none (0) opposing, none (0) abstaining and none (0) absent. (The Secretary-Treasurer does not vote and the Chairman votes only in case of a tie)

Suzie Fox
Recording Secretary

Roger Yankton Sr.
Chairman

Reed Soderstrom agreed to represent us pro-bono and went to work on a lawsuit against the NCAA and consulted with the tribe to make sure we were not out of line on any avenues we were going to pursue.

November 1st, 2011 in the tribal conference room, we held our press conference to announce our lawsuit against the NCAA. Even though only the local press attended the conference it was picked up by the national and international press.

A new phase had just begun and the new twists and turns the future was to bring was now un-stoppable and would bring us into contact with old foes as well as new ones.

CHAPTER 15:
IT NEVER SEEMS TO CHANGE

Here we go yet again, the roller coaster is still on a fast track and at times I wish I could get off, but if I want to be able to look into the mirror in the morning, I can't get off. The 12 count lawsuit has been filed and it's too late to turn back now.

Our lawsuit was filed on November 1st, 2011 plaintiffs (United States District Court for the Northeast Division, case # 2:11-CV-00095) and there was a press release. (see next page)

We met at the Spirit Lake Tribal Conference room in the Administration Building, what has become to be known as the (Blue Building). The full Tribal Council and all members of our committee were there as were our lawyers Reed Soderstrom, Stephen Behm and Gordon Caldis and announced that the lawsuit against the NCAA had been filed in Federal Court

As we sat behind the Tribal Council and the Attorneys, I could not help but wonder just what have we started now? What does this move have in store for us?

Although Chuck Haga from the Grand Forks Herald was there as well as Louise Oleson of the Devils Lake Journal, but the only one to give a fair reporting was Rob Port of Say Anything Blog.

PRESS CONFERENCE STATEMENT
NOVEMBER 1, 2011
SPIRIT LAKE SIOUX TRIBE

Today, November 1, 2011, the Spirit Lake Nation has filled a 10 count lawsuit vs. the NCAA, asking the Northeast Federal District Court to issue an immediate injunction on the policy banning and sanctioning the University of North Dakota from using the proud and honorable name, FIGHTING SIOUX.

The people of Spirit Lake have used dialogue and interaction with each other to fully examine all points of view regarding UND's use of the FIGHTING SIOUX name. Ultimately, the voice of the people of Spirit Lake was recognized by a vote held in April, 2009 that overwhelmingly approved UND's use of its name FIGHTING SIOUX.

The people of the Spirit Lake Sioux Nation were forced into this issue by an outside and foreign entity – the NCAA. The people of Spirit Lake have sent many letters and invitations to the NCAA to discuss this issue. The NCAA has either been unresponsive or has gone to the media to reassert a paternalistic and misguided policy that has resulted in the soiling a proud and honorable name by labeling FIGHTING SIOUX as "hostile" and "abusive".

Either by its intentional actions or by arrogance, the NCAA has muzzled the voice of brothers and sisters of the Standing Rock Sioux Tribe when over 1000 enrolled members of Standing Rock peacefully assembled and petitioned its government to hold a vote. The NCAA was silent when it came to the people of Standing Rock's right and desire to vote.

The NCAA policies, unfortunately like many policies forced upon American Indians throughout history, mandate and force compliance without any true understanding of Indian ways. Because of the history of "forced policies" upon Tribal Nations and specifically upon the Sioux, the NCAA's policy on UND's use of the FIGHTING SIOUX name is at best ignorant or at worst one more attempt to decimate and exterminate any memory of the plains Indians.

There is an inherent lack of any understanding of Sioux culture by the NCAA. It is believed the NCAA has no Indian Nations colleges in its ranks, no enrolled tribal member as an NCAA coach, no enrolled Indian tribal member in its administration, and few, if any enrolled members, participating in Division I NCAA athletics. These glaring NCAA deficiencies demonstrate that the NCAA should step aside and avoid trying to "help" Indian nations with policies that this Spirit Lake Tribe knows to have the opposite effect. The NCAA has never before demonstrated any empathy for plains Indians and lacks any moral high ground in its attempt to institute a unilateral policy on UND's use of the name FIGHTING SIOUX in this great state of North Dakota.

PRESS CONFERENCE STATEMENT
(TEXT AS FOLLOWS)

PRESS CONFERENCE STATEMENT
NOVEMBER 1, 2001
SPIRIT LAKE SIOUX TRIBE

Today, November 1, 2011, the Spirit Lake Nation has filed a 10 count lawsuit vs. the NCAA, asking the Northeast Federal District Court to issue an immediate injunction on the policy banning and sanctioning the University of North Dakota from using the proud and honorable name Fighting Sioux.

The people of Spirit Lake have used dialogue and interaction with each other to fully examine all points of view regarding UND's use of the Fighting Sioux name. Ultimately, the voice of the people of Spirit Lake was recognized by a vote held in April, 2009 that overwhelmingly approved UND's use of its name Fighting Sioux.

The people of the Spirit Lake Sioux Nation were forced into this issue by an outside and foreign entity- the NCAA. The people of Spirit Lake have many letters and invitations to the NCAA to discuss this issue. The NCAA has either been unresponsive or has gone to the media to reassert a paternalistic and misguided policy that has resulted in the soiling a proud and honorable name by labeling Fighting Sioux as "hostile" and "abusive".

Either by its intentional actions or by arrogance, the NCAA has muzzled the voice of brothers and sisters of the Standing Rock Sioux Tribe when over 1000 enrolled members of Standing Rock peacefully assembled and petitioned its government to hold a vote. The NCAA was silent when it came to the people of Standing Rock's right and desire to vote.

The NCAA policies, unfortunately like many other policies forced upon American Indians throughout history, mandate and force compliance without any true understanding of Indian ways. Because of the history of "forced policies" upon Tribal Nations and specifically upon the Sioux, the NCAA's policy on UND's use of the FIGHTING SIOUX name is at best ignorant or at worst one more attempt to decimate and exterminate any memory of the plains Indians.

There is an inherent lack of any understanding of Sioux culture by the NCAA. It is believed the NCAA has no Indian Nation colleges in its ranks, no enrolled tribal member as an NCAA coach, no enrolled Indian tribal member in its administration, and few, if any enrolled members, participating in Division I NCAA athletics. These glaring NCAA deficiencies demonstrate that the NCAA should step aside and avoid trying to "help" Indian nations with policies that this Spirit Lake Tribe knows to have the opposite effect. The NCAA has never before demonstrated any empathy for plains Indians and lacks any moral high ground on its institute a unilateral policy on UND's use of the name FIGHTING SIOUX in this great state of North Dakota.

IN THE UNITED STATES DISTRICT COURT
FOR THE DISTRICT OF NORTH DAKOTA
NORTHEASTERN DIVISION

The Spirit Lake Sioux Tribe of Indians, by)
and through its Committee of Understanding)
and Respect, and Archie Fool Bear, individually,)
and as Representative of the more than 1004)
Petitioners of the Standing Rock Sioux Tribe,)　　CASE NO.
　　　　　　　　　　　　　　　　　　　　　　　　　　　　　)
　　　　　　　　　　　　Plaintiffs,)
　　　　　vs.)
　　　　　　　　　　　　　　　　　　　　　　　　　　　　　)
The National Collegiate Athletic Association,)
　　　　　　　　　　　　Defendants.

COMPLAINT AND DEMAND FOR JURY TRIAL

Plaintiffs allege the following for their Complaint against Defendant National Collegiate Athletic Association (NCAA) by showing this honorable court as follows:

1.　　This Court has jurisdiction over this matter under 28 U.S.C. Sec. 1332, as the matter in controversy exceeds the sum of seventy-five thousand dollars, exclusive of interest and costs, and is between citizens or entities of different states. This court also has jurisdiction under 42 U.S.C. Sec. 1981, 1983,1988, 1996 and the 14th Amendment to the U.S. Constitution, the Sherman Act, 15 U.S.C. § 4, and 28 U.S.C. § 1331, 1337.

2.　　Venue is proper in this district under to 28 U.S.C. Sec. 1391(a) and 28 U.S.C. Sec. 1391.

JURISDICTION

3.　　Plaintiff Spirit Lake Tribe is a federally recognized American Indian tribe governed by a revised Constitution dated May 5, 1960, approved by Acting Commissioner, Bureau of Indian Affairs, July 14, 1961, and subsequently amended July 17, 1969; May 3,

OFFICIAL COMPLAINT FILING

TOP LEFT: FRANK BLACK CLOUD. TOP RIGHT: REED SODERSTUM
BOTTOM LEFT: JOHN CHASKE, BOTTOM RIGHT: ARCHIE FOOL BEAR

Frank Black Cloud spoke for our Committee as well as John
Chaske. Archie Fool Bear had made the trip from Standing Rock and
spoke; he was accompanied by a few other tribal members Joe
White Mountain, and his brother, and Antoine American Horse, a
spiritual leader who led the prayer before our announcement.

I don't know if I'm too sensitive on this subject, but in my opinion,
We were not taken serious. I had the feeling many in the news media
felt we were a joke.

But the normal occurrence stayed true to form and the opposition
views were sought more than ours. Our local reporter interviewed a
number of the opposition, but only nodded hello to supporters and
committee members. Then again, I've always had the view that most
media outlets love to cause controversy to create more of a story, and
this issue has given me more reason not to trust the majority of the

media. Sadly, the news media does not report the news but they attempt to create the news, just my opinion…

At the press release there was the same handful of out spoken individuals standing in the back of the room and shouting out threats and challenging the Tribal Councils authority to adopt the Resolution authorizing the Committee for Understanding and Respect to handle this issue. They also challenged the council over its authority to speak for tribal members. Although I didn't see Erich Longie in the room, it was said he was in the hall and gave interviews, but I didn't see him.

This was NOT a news conference, but just a press release. Although our attorney tried to answer a few of the questions posed by the small group of agitators, he finally told them that this was not a question and answer meeting, but if anyone wanted we would be available after the meeting to answer their questions.

Just days after our press release Erich Longie was on WDAZ -TV news, stating the Tribe has no authority to speak for "him" and the resolution on the Committee for Understanding and Respect as well as the lawsuit against the NCAA violates his tribal rights. In short, the Tribal Council does not have the authority to speak for tribal members, but on February 22nd, 2009 he said just the opposite in speaking to the ND State board committee. He said, "You have to talk only to the Tribal Government and not the people" when it was suggested the ND State board should meet with tribal members.

I thought hmmm….so it's not who you talk to, it's what they're going to say, so evidently you are supposed to only talk to people that agree with Mr. Longie or Tribal Government when they agree with Erich, again just my thoughts…

The agitators made a number of (what I thought were) idle threats about getting the Council and Chairman removed from office by any means necessary. But just has been the case since the Settlement/Agreement was signed in October of 2007, our local media has turned a blind eye to the tactics of the opposition leaders (Native as well as non-Native) and put their negative focus on supporters only.

News Reports have over the course of the last 4 years allowed false accusations of bribery, fraudulent names, intimidation, character assassinations, distortions, outright lies, and other baseless accusations against supporters go unchallenged. Yet the opposition leaders whether Native or not have had a free ride and allowed to do or say anything without any scrutiny.

Almost nothing has made it into the press about how much effort has been put into this issue by Native Americans, or just what has been accomplished by our tribe as well as members of Standing Rock.

We had come to expect this kind of news coverage so it did not surprise us and we took it in stride. We did not have the luxury of time to dwell on the coverage, for on November 7, 2011, we were back at the Capital to testify to Legislators again.

This time we are there to testify against SB 2370 a bill to repeal HB 1263 which had just passed months ago. Which, by the way still amazes me, just how a bill that was supported by so many, and not only the Native Americans but North Dakotans could be trashed and disregarded so easily.

The Special Session of Legislation was due to begin on November 11, 2011 and the combined ND House and Senate Education Committees convened on November 7th, to hear arguments for and against the proposed Legislation. This time the supporters of the Bill (Opposition to the name) were up first.

First up was Senator Laffen of district 43, who gave a forecast of doom and gloom because of the NCAA as well as the Big Sky Conference. He also shared a common theme that almost all the supporters of the bill expressed "I supported HB 1263 and I do not feel the name and logo is hostile or abusive, but I feel to keep it will hurt the University and it's athletic programs."

Next Senator O'Connell said, "It's time to put an end to the intimidation, it's time to put an end to the hostilities and bullying, it's time to put an end to the law we passed this spring"; he added, "we tried to bluff the NCAA and it didn't work."

I ask: So who are the intimidators? Who is the bully? Who is receiving the hostile treatment? Is it not you who has done these things in trying to bluff at a race of people's expense? Why? I ask myself, did these guys not stand with Spirit Lake? In researching, there are eight other universities that were given exemption with one tribe given their approval, with backing from that University as well as the state, why would North Dakota be any different. What the NCAA was allowed to do to North Dakota and Spirit Lake, would that not be discrimination and intimidation?

Then Rick Burgum stated he is a proud alumni member from 1968 and will always be a Fighting Sioux and every stone was turned to save the name and logo, but the price we will have to pay because of the NCAA and the Big Sky is too great. He says under NCAA sanction (1) either we retire the name and logo, or we will not be permitted to join the Big Sky Conference. That leads to many additional consequence, each of which is negative (2) with or without conference affiliations, other NCAA schools are officially discouraged from scheduling games with UND and those schools are following NCAA's precedence. (3) "Academically" there is a problem recruiting and retaining top quality faculty to our University.

I thought when I heard this; Why is this organization (NCAA) allowed to "bully" all of the colleges in this country and make them do as the NCAA Executive Committee says? Everything Rick Burgum just stated about 1, 2, and 3; sounds to me like a couple of bullies I had to deal with in elementary school and why do these Universities bow down to a few hypocrites? Burgum's # 1: I have a problem with his statement because the contract with the Big Sky was signed on October 26th, 2010 (we were in the Big Sky) and looking at the Big Sky agenda and the University of North Dakota was already on the football schedule through 2015 (WDAZ News April 28th, 2011).

Brian Faison UND Athletic Director was up and called for the repeal of HB 1263 and said that the Big Sky is an issue as well as NCAA sanctions, but he did not have a written statement so I can only go on memory. He also talked about the 80 years of traditions and how it will be respected.

Up next was Kylie Oversen, Student Body President. She truthfully states she does not represent the people of North Dakota or members of Spirit Lake or Standing Rock, but she claims she does represent the students of UND. She claims to have witnessed the negative effects on Native students. (The vast majorities are not of Sioux decent and are a minority of the Native American students at

163

UND). I thought if she truly was aware of any of this and represented the UND students why did she not do anything about it?

It was now President Kelley's turn and he advised the committee to just review the evidence and not to rely on anecdotes or rumors. He said, our membership in the Big Sky Conference is threatened by the NCAA sanctions. He said they will honor the 80 years of traditions and retire the name with dignity. He was asked again about the cost to retire and remove all reference to the Fighting Sioux, but just as he did 11 months ago, he gave no answer. He danced around the issue as if no one had ever thought about the subject in the last 3 years of trying desperately to get rid of it. Although he said it's not un-realistic to say he has spent half his time on this issue since arriving here in 2008.

Then come's Brittney Thomas a student of University of Mary who claims she would prefer the Fighting Sioux name to stay, but because of the NCAA and their sanctions as well as the Big Sky the name must go. Another thought "who the hell asked her to testify if she doesn't attend UND!!

She was followed by Erich Longie, who focused on the Committee for Understanding and Respect. Although it is not in his written testimony he did challenge a member of the Tribal Council who was in attendance at the hearing. He talked about only 10% of Spirit Lake voted in the primary of 2009; that the vast majority opposes the name and logo, and that they have yet another petition circulating on the reservation. Again it never gets enough signatures. In a written statement provided to the committee, he attacked the Tribal Council and our committee with many accusations that boarder on slander.
In his written testimony many accusations are made.

I. It claims that two committee members have been involved/ and or convicted of stealing money from Spirit Lake tribe, or from the US Government. At least one member has served prison time. Another has been convicted of a crime regarding tribal funds.

II. Qualifications for tribal council, is not to have been convicted of a Felony.

III. How do we know the committee is not misusing funds raised so far?

IV. The committee has taken the authority to say or do whatever they feel like, also that the committee is denying tribal members the right to speak and called members of the opposition half breeds.

V. That one committee member was raised off the reservation and only returned 15 years ago, he has no right to speak.

VI. The NCAA has not attacked our culture or way of life.

VII. Both UND and the ND State board have said they don't want our name.

VIII. As a tribe we don't call ourselves Sioux.

IX. The committee has involved the whole tribe into their personal fight.

It must be pointed out that Erich claims to speak for the majority but has never been able to muster enough support to submit even one legitimate petition to back up his cause. As to a comment about half breeds by one of his supporters, Erich himself is one, he can supply no proof to his supposed majority, cause there is none, but I (a full blood enrolled member) was told by his supporters that I had no right because I was just a foster kid. He fails to mention it was the NCAA and UND that involved us in to this fight through the Settlement/Agreement not the other way around.

Up now is Jesse Taken Alive, and he starts again by speaking in the Lakota language for a few minutes. He again talks about de-colonization and de-humanization. He refers to all the resolutions signed by him and a handful of others. It was almost word for word of his testimony in January and March of this year.

Now it was our turn:
We started again with John Chaske. He again states the true facts that have carried this issue to this point. Our Committee for Understanding and Respect was organized at the request of tribal elders in 2007, that we were officially appointed to represent 67% of members who voiced their support for the name and logo. We take great pride in our Sioux culture and heritage. Today, we stand in

defense of our proud name that has been declared hostile and abusive by the NCAA.

Then we have Frank Black Cloud an enrolled member of Spirit Lake, first thanked the citizen and leaders in North Dakota for the courage to stand against the NCAA when they passed the law keeping the Fighting Sioux, it showed they heard the voice of the Sioux people, that unfortunately been silenced. It was a gutsy stand. He also mentioned some quotes from some of our famous leaders like Sitting Bull who said "We never picked up the pen, we weren't invited, just told what was good for us" and Red Cloud who said "Only the white man's language can make right wrong and wrong right". Contrary to "beliefs" the name and logo has help heal the years of hostility between our cultures.

Followed by me, Eunice Davidson "Goodstar Woman"; I talked about my pride in who I am as a Dakota Sioux woman. I talked about the pride our tribal members have shown in their vote as well as how much Fighting Sioux apparel you will see on not just our reservation but all over the country.

Archie is up next and informed the committee of certain facts. For years the Government has developed policies and tried to do away with Indian Nations. Policies were developed to terminate, relocate, and assimilate us into mainstream society to take away our land, and to do away with our heritage, our culture and way of life. Over 140 years ago our ancestors had the foresight and seen the need for us to hang on to our way of life, our culture, our values and our homeland and against their beliefs signed a treaty establishing the Great Sioux Nation. Then 42 years ago tribal leaders having a similar foresight sent leaders to UND and bestowed the name to the University. He talked about how a small group of tribal members tried to change Standing Rock's name from the "Sioux", but it was shot down overwhelmingly. He provided the proof that the 1969 ceremony did in "fact" take place.

Then David was up and again he had a blistering statement. Just as he did in January and March at the House and Senate hearings. He attacked the opposition, ND State board and UND Administration for the false and misleading information and testimony. He started off with official Government statistics that showed the number of eligible voters on Spirit Lake and just how over 90% of them turned out to vote in 2009 primary and of which 67% voted to keep the name and logo. Spirit Lake was not evenly divided as it has been represented.

He then produced the signed contract between UND and the Big Sky from October of 2010 and clearly the Big Sky would be in breach of a legal contract if they removed UND. He also showed strong evidence that the Big Sky needed UND more than UND needed the Big Sky. He provided the proof of just what the NCAA sanctions truly are and that the exaggeration are just that, exaggerations meant to scare the Legislators into turning their backs on the Sioux people as well as citizens of North Dakota.

Renita DeLorme spoke of how as a full blood and older than average student at UND, the white students showed nothing but respect to her and even went out of their way to help her. She added that to repeal the law would say the stories of UND being "a hostile and abusive environment" are true and that would be tragic.

Next a tribal youth enrolled member and a high school student. Told about her desire to attend UND as her Grandmother was the first generation graduate of UND and her father was the second generation and her dream was to be third, which will be in jeopardy if the name goes.

Marilyn Schoenberg added testimony and a written statement, which has been a staunch supporter and has written a couple of letters to the Grand Forks Herald.

This ended the testimony to the joint committee and the meeting was adjourned. The joint committees were going to meet in separate sessions to make their recommendation to the full "House and Senate" Legislators. In their closed session amendments were discussed and voted on. The one important amendment was that no new name could be chosen till 2015 as to give a "cooling off period".

The full texted can be found at.
http://www.legis.nd.gov/files/resource/62-2011/library/sb2370.pdf?201308071550004

Another troubling tactic in the opposition's on going war against Native Americans is their apparent use of the public funds in their lobbying efforts, this, under North Dakota law is illegal and prohibited.   Not being an attorney, I don't know all the legal language of the law, but the question of using State owned vehicles (cars and air planes) to transport individuals to lobby against the name and image came up a number of times.

One such story was in the Grand Forks Herald on March 11, 2011 which states that planes owned by UND's Aerospace Foundation were used to transport staff and students to testify to the State Legislators against the name and image. This would be illegal under ND Law.

Then again on June 5th, 2012 five coaches along with UND's athletic director on a two day lobbying sweep of the State against the name and image flew from Fargo to Bismarck in a plane leased by NDSU, upon landing in Bismarck they were informed that this was illegal. But instead of arranging new transportation from that point on, they chose to continue on to Minot then to Grand Forks and back to Fargo.

Although the story leaked out, it was quickly swept under the carpet and goes nowhere.

On November 8th, 2011 the day after we testified to the joint Senate and House Education Committees, unknown to us, the anti-name and logo people were allowed to give more testimony on the final bill wording. Senator Flakoll who appears to be against the name and logo for personal reasons (my opinion) wanted the name and logo to disappear as soon as the new law passes, should it pass. There were Legislators who recognized to do so would pour salt in the wound of many North Dakotans not to mention Spirit Lake and the actual Sioux who have been fighting so hard to keep it in place.

Leading up to the special session there was talk of a "three year" moratorium on any new name as a cooling off period. This was discussed at length during the hearing, and the legislators questioned members of the ND State board on the subject. A few of the Legislators mentioned that they are receiving e-mails asking them not to repeal the current law.

Representative ReAnn Kelsch (co-Chairman) of the joint committee even expressed concerns that the ND State board, and UND Administration would keep their word on a "three year" moratorium and that it must be put in writing of the new law, to which ND State board member Duane Espergard expressed disappointment that she would not trust them. I thought, this man just cannot see how transparent he has been, in showing his bias on the issue and not supporting the Fighting Sioux name and logo, after hearing and seeing him attack Sam Dupris at the Dickinson meeting, just strengthens my opinion that his tunnel vision is just that. He can't see beyond his own wants!

There was discussion on what happens if Spirit Lake wins their lawsuit. If they win the cost of changing everything at UND would not be necessary. Now President of the ND State board Grant Shaft said there still would be possible road blocks to re-instating the name. Even if the NCAA were to lift the sanction he suggested that whatever conference we may get into may have their own policy against names and logos. I thought what about the Iowa "Hawkeyes", the Central Michigan "Chippewa's", and the Seminoles? I wonder who has rejected them due to their name and logo?

But on November 8th, 2011 the House Education Committee voted 15 to 0 to recommend DO PASS to the full House and the Senate voted 6 for and none against with 1 absent. On it went to both houses with a "do pass" recommendation.

The full House and Senate wasted no time in turning their backs on the citizens of North Dakota whether Sioux or not. The House voted 63 to 31 in favor of SB 2370 and the Senate voted 39 to 7 in favor of SB 2370 on November 9th, 2011. The governor was also ready with pen in hand on November 9th, 2011.

I would like to express my gratitude to the 31 House members and 7 Senators who stood on principle and have values, but for the rest, my opinion of them can't be expressed in words that could pass moral muster. What I truly believe is that most of those to vote in favor of SB 2370 are Bigots, Racist, or just plain Politicians, with but one objective "pretend you have values so as to get re-elected." That as Sioux people we mean nothing to them and are of no consequence unless useful for further individual political gains.

The "three year" moratorium gave cover to them. They now can say to their constituents; we didn't vote against the name and logo, but just for more time. This to please the supporters of the name, they can say to the opposition we voted against keeping the name and logo. This takes an issue out of upcoming elections and helps their re-election chances.

The new law means we have to regroup yet again.

Chapter 16:
North Dakotans Speak!

What next? Where do we go from here? I think a refresher course is needed again. I'm sure many of you are by now asking "Why do they keep putting themselves in turmoil?" so we have to go back to the beginning again.

I know it seems as though I am rehashing old news, but even for me, it's hard to remember all that has happened and I lived through it. I'm only stating hi-lights to show what I believe are a pattern of deceit along with some of the new facts we found.

In 1883, the University of North Dakota was founded even before we were a State, which didn't happen until 1889. Until then we were Dakota Territory because it was the Dakota Tribes territory and not a state. The sports teams started off with NoDak's and Flickertail (After the state rodent). After a number of years they found it hard to generate enthusiasm for those names and searched for a new nickname, one that would be more representative of a proud history.

In 1930, the students at the University of North Dakota which were mainly descendants of the state's early pioneers recognized the heartiness and stamina of their parents and grandparents as well as the earlier inhabitants (The Dakota Sioux) and said what could be more fitting, and they talked to the tribes and UND Sioux was born.

In 1969 after 40 years of use to cement the name and education opportunities a Sacred Ceremony was performed at UND where the

171

name was bestowed for eternity by members of Standing Rock and Devils Lake Sioux (Spirit Lake). The name was bestowed to insure educational opportunities as well as honoring our ancestors.

From 1969 till the present day, the number of Native American programs at UND has grown. UND now has more Native American programs than any other major University.

In the 1980's a small group of Native Americans students at UND with the aid of some of the professors at Merrifield Hall started a group call S.O.A.R (Students Organized Against Racism) and then later called B.R.I.D.G.E.S (Building Roads Into Diverse Groups Empowering Students), before this issue happened you could go into the University of North Dakota's web site and find information on their stance on the name and symbol, but they seem to be phrasing them out now. It appears they are of no more use..

Something new that we found was an article from November 28th, 2007, a month after the Settlement was signed. In which the Chairman of Standing Rock says "any attempts to save the name and image would be a waste of time" and he goes on to say "the name should be changed to the Rough Riders" in honor of Teddy Roosevelt. The interesting thing here is that we have heard rumors that high ranking State officials had also inquired about the name with a local school using that name at the same time. We know there was communications between the Chairman and ND State board, UND, and the State Attorney General and the NCAA. Was this a plan from the beginning? Just more of my thoughts…

February 1st, 2008 Grand Forks Herald: has a story that Spirit Lake may hold a referendum (vote) on UND and the nickname. Chairwoman Myra Pearson says she would support such a vote, but she personally opposes the name and image. Was the response to council member (Lois Leben) for a tribe wide vote.

The enrolled members of Spirit Lake take great pride in our ancestors and even with knowledge of the past atrocities perpetrated on them by corrupt politicians as well as trading post owners and such, we know of the broken treaties, we know of the total theft of all our lands through deceit, we know of the intentional distorted description painted of our ancestors by so-called honest journalists, we know of the murder of our ancestors by greedy land speculators, we know all this and more, but had hoped those days of treachery had passed only to find it continues to this day.

The Fighting Sioux name and image is not just a gimmick for a University, it is a healing of past injustices, it is a sense of pride to most Native Americans, it is a picture of a proud and fierce people that fought against overwhelming odds. It has become educational opportunities; it has become a belief that our voice has meaning. It is not a white kid painted up to be an Indian riding a horse and throwing a flaming spear into the ground, it is a proud image of a proud people, not just Sioux. It is an honorable image of a race of people that still exist in spite of all the efforts to exterminate them and their culture.

We have come to believe that, we have been used again by the powerful, but we are determined to fight to the end. Fight on we must, or we will be forgotten like so many other tribes. This is no longer just about a "name" but has advanced to a battle against an effort of intentional genocide of a race of people. It cannot be tolerated.

I don't want to be so judgmental but sadly our society has become about appearances rather than truth. We are going backwards rather than forward in time. The only thing that has changed is the names of the corrupt, they still for their own personal gain manipulating and distorting truth.

Then you have those in the white community that because of political correctness find a need to make us Indians nothing more than helpless children and that we are too stupid to know what is good for us. They do more damage than any other group because they have no knowledge of what an Indian is, they just think they do.

But here we are, we must either, give in to the powers that be, and become good little Indians following orders or move to another step in what seems to be a never ending struggle for respect. There is only one way to proceed. Now we must fight for the rights of all the citizens of North Dakota, but now we enter a new phase with no illusions of who we are fighting against. We are going to rely on good and honest citizens of the State and we have confidence in their support.

PETITION TITLE

This referendum measure would reject Senate Bill 2370 as passed by the Legislature in the November 2011 Special Session and printed below. Senate Bill 2370 repealed section 15-10-46 of the North Dakota Century Code which had required that the Fighting Sioux nickname and logo be used by the University of North Dakota.

FULL TEXT OF THE MEASURE

IF MATERIAL IS UNDERSCORED, IT IS NEW MATERIAL WHICH IS BEING ADDED. IF MATERIAL IS OVERSTRUCK BY DASHES, THE MATERIAL IS BEING DELETED. IF MATERIAL IS NOT UNDERSCORED OR OVERSTRUCK, THE MATERIAL IS EXISTING LAW THAT IS NOT BEING CHANGED.

Senate Bill 2370

AN ACT relating to adoption of a nickname and logo for the university of North Dakota athletic teams; to repeal section 15-10-46 of the North Dakota Century Code, relating to the university of North Dakota fighting Sioux nickname and logo; and to provide an effective date.

BE IT ENACTED BY THE LEGISLATIVE ASSEMBLY OF NORTH DAKOTA:

SECTION 1.UNIVERSITY OF NORTH DAKOTA ATHLETIC NICKNAME AND LOGO. Neither the state board of higher education nor the university of North Dakota may adopt or implement an athletic nickname or corresponding logo before January 1, 2015.

SECTION 2.REPEAL. Section 15-10-46 of the North Dakota Century Code is repealed.

SECTION 3.EFFECTIVE DATE. This Act becomes effective on December 1, 2011.

INSTRUCTIONS TO PETITION SIGNERS

You are being asked to sign a petition. You must be a qualified elector. This means you are eighteen years old, you have lived in North Dakota thirty days, and you are a United States citizen. All signers must add their complete residential address or rural route or general delivery address and the date of signing. Every qualified elector signing a petition must do so in the presence of the individual circulating the petition.

QUALIFIED ELECTORS

Month, Day, Year	Name of Qualified Elector	Residential Address or Complete Rural Route or General Delivery Address	City, State Zip Code

2011 PETITION (TEXT AS FOLLOWS)

PETITION TITLE

This referendum measure would reject Senate Bill 2370 as passed by the Legislature in the November 2011 Special Session and printed below. Senate Bill 2370 repealed section 15-10-46 of the North Dakota Century Code which had required that the Fighting Sioux nickname and logo be used by the University of North Dakota.

FULL TEXT OF THE MEASURE

IF MATERIAL IS UNDERSCORED, IT IS NEW MATERIAL WHICH IS BEING ADDED. IF MATERIAL IS OVERSTRUCK BY DASHES, THE MATERIAL IS BEING DELETED. IF MATERIAL IS NOT UNDERSCORED OR OVERSTRUCK, THE MATERIAL IS EXISTING LAW THAT IS NOT BEING CHANGED.

174

Senate Bill 2370

AN ACT relating to adoption of a nickname and logo for the University of North Dakota athletic teams; to repeal section 15-10-46 of the North Dakota Century Code, relating to the University of North Dakota fighting Sioux nickname and logo; and to provide an effective date.

BE IT ENACTED BY THE LEGISLATIVE ASSEMBLY OF NORTH DAKOTA

SECTION 1. UNIVERSTITY OF NORTH DAKOTA ATHLETIC NICKNAME AND LOGO. *Neither the state board of higher education nor the University of North Dakota may adopt or implement an athletic nickname or corresponding logo before January 1, 2015.*

SECTION 2. REPEAL. Section 15-10-46 of the North Dakota Century Code is repealed.

SECTION 3. EFFECTIVE. *This Act becomes effective on December 1,*

INSTRUCTIONS TO PETITION SIGNERS

You are being asked to sign a petition. You must be a qualified elector. This means you are eighteen years old, you have lived in North Dakota thirty days, and you are a United States citizen. All signers must add their complete residential address or rural route or general delivery address and the date of signing. Every qualified elector signing a petition must do so in the presence of the individual circulating the petition.

On December 16th, 2011 we get approval from the Secretary of State, Al Jaeger for a Statewide petition for a vote to repeal the repeal law. We also get approval for a second petition to put it into the North Dakota Constitution.

We will have 53 days to get required signatures (13,452) to put the issue on the June 2012 primary ballot. Normally, a petition gives up to 90 days, but it must be turned in so many days before the vote, in our case due to the lateness of passage of SB 2370 (Repeal Law) we had to scramble just to get a petition made up and registered sponsors for the petition. We submitted our paperwork on December 1st, 2011 but it was not officially approved till December 14th, 2011, and had to be done by February 7th, 2012.

We have 50 individuals registered as sponsors for the petition to repeal the repeal, which would be placed on the ballot of the June 2012 primary election if enough signatures could be gathered.

The petition to put it into the State Constitution required over 27,000, signature and we would have till December of 2012, so our focus was on the repeal with which we had less than two months.

In the weeks leading up to the petition drive, we had a number of conference calls with committee members and our new "friends" including a few lawyers. One of whom suggested we talk to an individual who had worked on a Presidential campaign. We were able to have this person join one of our conference calls. He told us something we were starting to realize. He said it does not matter how much truth and honor you have on your side, it is how you frame the debate. He said an ad campaign would cost close to $80,000.00 dollars if you want to succeed. We would have to choose words and our focus carefully. Again, he stated truth is of little importance, it's how you state it. We thought we understood but got a real education in the months to come.

The consultant also informed us that the standard charge was $2.50 for a signature on a petition. We needed 13,500 signatures that would cost us $32500.00 and when you add the media campaign of $80,000.00 you're looking at least $112,000.00 and then there would need to be a survey done at another cost of $25,000.00 HOLY ****!!! We at this point had about a thousand dollars in donations committed to Save the Fighting Sioux.com

Our petitions were given little chance for success by those in power, and I think they laughed about this little group of stupid Indians out there on the frozen prairie, but eventually they woke up and we found out just what the consultant was forecasting for us to encounter, but now I'm getting ahead of myself.

Our first organized signing event was on December 30 and 31, 2011. We were somewhat surprised that the REA who had stood with us through the journey so far, would not break policy to allow us in the building to get signatures on the petition to save the interior of the building as well as the Fighting Sioux name and image. How ironic!

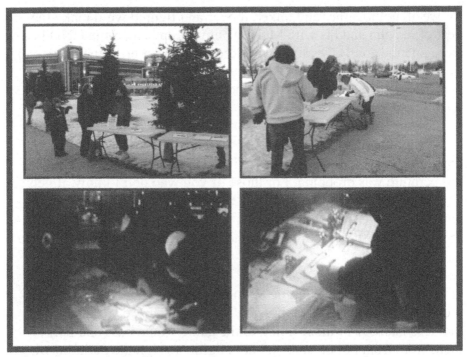

TOP: GETTING SIGNATURES OUTSIDE THE RALPH IN THE BACKGROUND. TEMPERATURES 5 ABOVE, BUT BELOW 0 WIND-CHILL
BOTTOM: OUTSIDE THE RAPLH AND BOOKSTORE ON THE UND CAMPUS GETTING SIGNATURES. WELL BELOW 0 WIND-CHILL TEMP

The lawyer that stood with us fighting in District court in 2009, North Dakota Supreme Court in 2010, was now on the other side standing with the Engelstad Foundation fighting us in court on December 29th, 2011 to deny accessibility. As they said and which is true, the Engelstad Foundation has a policy of not allowing any protests or Political advisee groups on the property. Their reasoning "if you allow one you have to allow all". But they would clear snow off a couple of spots for us off their property

December 30th, 2011 we arrive around 4:30 PM, two and a half hours before the UND Fighting Sioux were to play Harvard in hockey. We looked up Jody Hodsgon (General Manager of the Engelstad Arena) and were shown just where we could set up our stands.

We were surprised and disappointed in the locations we were allowed to set up at, both locations were in the dark and out of the traffic. But what could we do? Poor places were better than no place.

So we all got together and talked it over and figured we'd make the best of it. John and his wife Mona would set up behind the UND book store and me and Dave along with Reed would set up at the north end of the arena. Both locations were well over 100 yards from the entrance to the arena, in the dark and the least traveled by fans, but what could we do?

It was about 5:30 PM when we started collecting signatures and the game would start at 7:00 PM. The sun was going down and the temperature was dropping. For those of you who don't know, it gets cold in the North Dakota Winters. By the time the sun was down the temperature was around +5 degrees and with the wind chill it was around -10 degrees. It was one of the warmer nights we would have to encounter.

As we stood there hanging on to our petitions so they wouldn't blow away, the fans started passing by. Although we were in a spot that less than 5% of those going to the game would pass and half of them were from out of state and not eligible to sign the petition, we were confident. (You had to be a citizen of North Dakota for 6 months before being eligible to vote).

Even as cold as it was our hearts were warm, for as the fans passed by they yelled encouragement to us. We had fans of hockey, from Harvard who could not understand what was happening here. They always look forward to every chance to play the Fighting Sioux and why would anybody want to change such a proud name? At least a third of those to pass by were from Minnesota and they supported our efforts and wished they could sign.

We would call John and Mona on our cell phone to see how they were doing and he would say that hardly anybody was passing there. He was located behind the bookstore and in a darker place than us, but his spirit was high in spite of the cold and being hidden.

About 6:00 PM we heard this bull horn yelling out "sign the petition here" and wondered who that was. Reed who had just gotten back from moving the Fighting Sioux camper due to orders from campus police said it was Charles.

Charles and Bella in Jamestown, ND.
(Courtesy of the AP)

Charles Tuttle is a professional advocate. He had been on some of our conference calls, but we had never met him. But looking over to the front of the bookstore here was this funny little man with a top hat and a big dog shouting into a bull horn. Dave just had to walk over to get a better look.

When he returned he said Charles seems to know what he is doing. Charles said he has done petitions for Ohio State University and in California but he studies state laws before beginning to make sure he is legal.

In North Dakota, the law says that you have access to any public facility. He said, if state funds are used by these originations they must give you access. He was set up in front of the Bookstore and although they complained he had pointed out the law and they gave in. Charles wanted to meet some place after we quit for the evening and I thought that would be great just to thaw out.

It was about 7:45 PM when we started packing up. We all met at the Bookstore and decided to go to Perkins for coffee and something to eat. While enjoying the warmth, we talked over the events of the night.

As I said this was the first time we met Charles and Bella in person. Charles is kind of short and a little over weight; he is quite cute with his top hat, full length wool trench coat and big cigar hanging out of his mouth. But the star of the evening was Bella, a very large Italian mastiff wearing a Fighting Sioux jersey, we would come to know both Charles and Bella very well over the coming months.

As I said Charles does this kind of work for a living and is very knowledgeable about the laws in whatever state he is working in. Knowing our financial situation and believing in our cause, he agreed to gather petitions and payment would be based on our donations received. He had started just as soon as the State had officially recognized our petition on December 14th, 2011 and had been challenged a number of times already. He has been challenged by security from the University, state funded Alerus Center, The REA and others, but carrying a copy of the state law was able to stifle these institutions, with the threat of suing if arrested.

The security guards and even policy officers would explain they are only carrying out orders and many even signed the petition.

It was clear that the establishment was going to make our efforts as difficult as possible. We had to fight the harsh North Dakota winters (Average temperatures of 20 below zero), The Grand Forks Herald and (what we feel was biased reporting), lack of financing, limited time, and now we are told to stand in the dark or out on the prairie.

But all this did was strengthen our resolve; we had a number of businesses throughout the state that had agreed to allow our petition there. We were at every UND hockey game getting signatures and sat at all most every public event getting more signatures. Yes, we had to be outside in the cold but that did not detour us. Dave even snuck into a Lake Region Community College basketball game at the sports center even after the Superintendent of Devils Lake Public denied access.

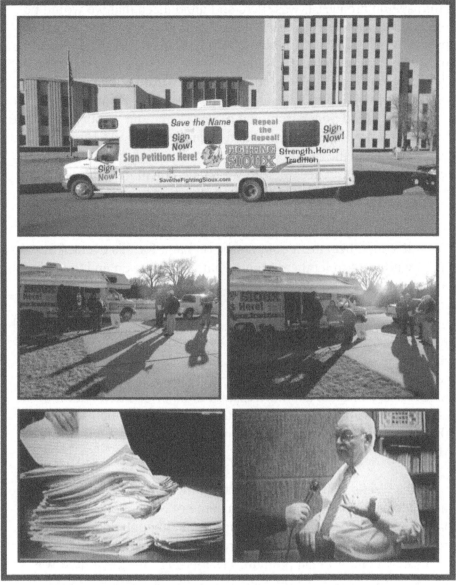

TOP: Sioux RV at the State Capitol for petition signing.
CENTER: At the Capitol, February 6th, 2011
BOTTOM LEFT: Petitions turned in February 2011
BOTTOM RIGHT: Al Jagger Secretary of State

But the big day arrived February 7th, 2012, and we had the Fighting Sioux camper parked outside of the Capital Building, of Bismarck

Radio station broadcast, was there and announced that we would be collecting signatures till 7:00 PM and had a notary present to stamp any forms necessary. Members of our Committee for Understanding and Respect were on hand, included were John Chaske, Frank Black Cloud & Courtney Black Cloud, Eunice Davidson & Dave Davidson, Sr., Archie Fool Bear, Don Barcome, Pam Brekke, Sean Johnson, and our attorney Reed Soderstrom and of course the star of our committee Bella Gabriella (Italian Mastiff) and Charles Tuttle. As Eunice and Pam were inside the Siouxper RV going over all the signatures to make one more last check before we handed them in to the Secretary of State's office. This is the first time I have ever been involved with anything of this magnitude and it was interesting, and I was kind of nervous but felt good about being involved. As some of our committee members that could not be on hand for this event. I always talked with them to let them know what was going on and they always gave their approval.

It was around 9:00 PM when we entered the Capital Building with our petitions. In all we had over 17,000 signatures well above the requirement of "13,500". As Archie, Dave, Reed and Sean carried in the boxes of petitions we felt exuberant that we had DONE IT. The ND Secretary of State and his assistant did a brief examination of the petitions and said they would have to do a full exam then send out 2000 inquiries at random to verify signatures, once done it would be official.

In the weeks leading up to February, the opposition made claims of unattended petitions lying around at some of our outlets and claims that people had been pressured to sign, and although no proof was provided, a number of petitions were rejected. Then there were some names they couldn't read or addresses missing. By the time it was done we still had over 15,000 signatures. My husband was one of those to receive a verification notice.

But the name and symbol was back in place and we now waited for our hearing in Federal District Court against the NCAA in April, were back in business again.

Chapter 17: The Court & Media

I hate to say it again but we thought we could breathe again. We knew the work was not done, but at least we now had a breathing spell. We had 10 months to collect the necessary signatures for the initiated measure to put the issue in the ND Constitution. We have our court date with the NCAA in April; we had the state wide primary vote in June. Sure, we knew it was not going to be clear sailing from this point on, but with all the obstacles that had been put in front of us and the overwhelming response from citizens of North Dakota gave us all the confidence needed and we moved on to the second petition drive.

February 15th, 2012: we were in Fargo for a news conference. We had scheduled this news conference a week earlier. The press knew and even a reporter from Chicago NPR (National Public Radio) was there along with local news outlets, to hear just what our plans were. We felt good about successfully getting the issue on the upcoming primary ballet on June 12th, 2012. Now we had to get the message out about the importance of putting the issue on the November, general election and in to the State Constitution.

We wanted to keep the message on positive accomplishments that had been achieved and avoid anything negative. It was the fight by the Sioux people that had brought this issue this far and we were to speak of the honor we felt through the use of our name and likeness. How proud we are of our ancestors.

PETITION TITLE

This initiated measure would add a new section to article VIII of the North Dakota Constitution providing that the University of North Dakota and its intercollegiate athletic teams shall be known as the "Fighting Sioux."

FULL TEXT OF THE MEASURE

IF MATERIAL IS UNDERSCORED, IT IS NEW MATERIAL WHICH IS BEING ADDED. IF MATERIAL IS OVERSTRUCK BY DASHES, THE MATERIAL IS BEING DELETED. IF MATERIAL IS NOT UNDERSCORED OR OVERSTRUCK, THE MATERIAL IS EXISTING LAW THAT IS NOT BEING CHANGED.

BE IT ENACTED BY THE PEOPLE OF THE STATE OF NORTH DAKOTA:

SECTION 1. A new section to Article VIII of the Constitution of North Dakota is created and enacted as follows:

The University of North Dakota and its intercollegiate athletic teams shall be known as the "Fighting Sioux".

INSTRUCTIONS TO PETITION SIGNERS

You are being asked to sign a petition. You must be a qualified elector. This means you are eighteen years old, you have lived in North Dakota thirty days, and you are a United States citizen. All signers must add their complete residential address or rural route or general delivery address and the date of signing. Every qualified elector signing a petition must do so in the presence of the individual circulating the petition.

QUALIFIED ELECTORS

Month, Day Year	Name of Qualified Elector	Residential Address or Complete Rural Route or General Delivery Address	City, State Zip Code

SECOND PETITION (TEXT AS FOLLOWS)

PETITION TITLE

This initiated measure would add a new section to article VIII of the North Dakota Constitution providing that the University of North Dakota and its intercollegiate teams shall be known as the "Fighting Sioux."

FULL TEXT OF THE MEASURE

IF MATERIAL IS UNDERSCORED, IT IS NEW MATERIAL, WHICH IS BEING ADDED. IF MATERIAL IS OVERSTRUCK BY DASHES, THE MATERIAL IS BEING DELETED, IF MATERIAL IS NOT UNDERSCORED OR OVERSTRUCK, THE MATERIAL IS EXISTING LAW THAT IS NOT BEING CHANGED.

BE IT ENACTED BY THE PEOPLE OF THE STATE OF North Dakota:

Section1. A new section to Article VIII of the Constitution of North Dakota is created and enacted as follows;

The University of North Dakota and its intercollegiate teams shall be known as the "Fighting Sioux".

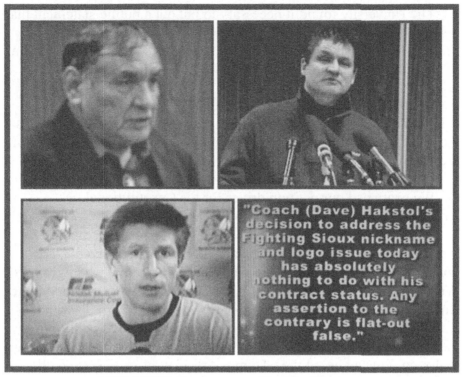

"Coach (Dave) Hakstol's decision to address the Fighting Sioux nickname and logo issue today has absolutely nothing to do with his contract status. Any assertion to the contrary is flat-out false."

TOP LEFT: JOHN AT OUR PRESS RELEASE
TOP RIGHT: FRANK BURGGARF AT OUR PRESS RELEASE
BOTTOM LEFT: COACH DAVE HASKEL (COURTESY OF WDAZ)
BOTTOM RIGHT: UND'S STATEMENT (COURTESY OF FOX NEWS)

In the middle of our news conference, as John was speaking, a reporter came rushing back in, and asked how we felt about the hockey Coach just now coming out in favor of retiring the name and image? Rather surprised with this new turn of events, and not sure how to respond, John asked our new "friend" Frank Burggraf to respond.

Frank is a UND Alumni, and a proud former UND hockey player. He started off with a few things must be pointed out here. Our news conference had been scheduled for over a week, but UND, and the coach decided to hold an unscheduled conference at the same time as ours. It is also worth noting the coach's contract that normally would have been offered and signed months ago was just now being signed, and he gets a substantial raise. He then asked for everyone to make up their own minds as to "why now?"

185

The University found it necessary to put out a public statement that his contract had nothing to do with his new position now on the Fighting Sioux issue. Needless to say, it got more coverage than us on the nightly news

It must also be pointed out that at the "10" year anniversary celebration of the "REA" a few months earlier the coach said: he was then and will always be a Fighting Sioux, we have to just take them at their word as to the New Position.

We continued our petition drives for the Constitutional Amendment at the public events and other outlets.

During our early fund raising campaign we had received a large donation, and the individual had pledged all the money we might need. We suggested there would be push back from the University and State Board, he had responded with: "It's my money and I can do with it as I want, they can't scare me" but when our donors list was published in the paper in a negative way, his as well as many other donations were to dry up. We had heard the "Alumni Association" was putting all kinds of pressure on would be donors. We didn't know if it was true or not, but something clearly was happening.

We were now coming to the belief, there must be some very powerful individuals or groups out there intimidating any would be supporters. We had hoped to have some money for an ad campaign by now, but instead we were in the hole. The many rich donors, that had indicated their full support, were now reduced to just verbal support in secret. Our constant travel to petition signing events was becoming a strain on all our personal pocket books, but we had come too far to quit now. We had won all the open battles, only to have sneaky and underhanded tactic's "thwart us". It seemed like we were fighting a group of terrorists, it was like Guerilla warfare where you never know just who, and where the enemy was. We knew we couldn't trust the ND State Board, or UND Administration, and now we are not sure, of the Legislators and the courts as well.

TOP LEFT: DEVIL'S LAKE PARK
TOP RIGHT: BISMARCK CIVIC CENTER
CENTER (LEFT TO RIGHT): TURTTLE MOUNTAIN RESERVATION,
JAMESTOWN RIB FEST, AT THE FARGO DOOM RIB FEST
BOTTOM: BEN BRIEN (THE ARTIST THAT CREATED THE UND LOGO)
AT BELCOURT ON TURTTLE MOUNTAIN

The one bright light was the everyday citizens, not just North Dakotans, but almost everyone we talked to. There was one such case while doing a petition signing event at West Acres in Fargo, when about "30" enrolled member of Sisseton tribe, in South Dakota had heard about the event and drove over a "100" miles to sign the petition. Sadly we had to tell them only North Dakota residents were eligible. This issue crosses racial, sexual, religious, and any other barriers. Of the thousands of people we met, I would say almost all took offence to the NCAA, and their dictatorship ways, but all were totally amazed to find out what we had faced from the State Board and UND Administration.

But on we went just like the ever-ready battery, and by the time we reach the Federal Court date April 21st, 2012, we had close to "22,000" signatures on the initiated measure, and our goal of 30,000 signatures was well within reach.

We entered the court room; there was I and Dave along with, Frank Black Cloud, John Chaske, and LaVonne Alberts from Spirit Lake, and then, Archie Fool Bear, Anton American Horse and another member from Standing Rock. We also had some of our new white friends there also. Reed Soderstrom, Stephen Behm, and Gordon Caldis, were the attorney's to present our case as to why this lawsuit should go forward, and it should be heard by a jury, and not just a judge, as requested in our brief.

Jonathan Duncan, was representing the NCAA, and had someone else from the "NCAA" seated at the table with him. From our point of view: the only one to support them, and the NCAA, was maybe Chuck Haga of the Grand Forks Herald.

We did not have a good feeling, because just days before this, the same Federal Judge, we are facing, had denied our request for sealed documents from the 2006, North Dakota lawsuit. Documents we *believed* would clearly show prior knowledge by the NCAA, and North Dakota AG, that the terms of the Settlement/Agreement could and would never be met. Resulting in putting, "Spirit Lake Tribal members, as well as Standing Rock members" out there to be ridiculed, slandered, and worse, going through with what these people knew would be a waste of time. They apparently did all of this, intending to preserve a false image for the elites of actually caring about Native Americans.

The "Dismissal Hearing", started off just as we feared, the Judge interrupted our attorney, who was up first, and right from the start, posed scenarios that "werenʼt" even thought up by the NCAA. Our attorney was never allowed to present our full argument, or just about any of what his brief had in it. The judge suggested our lawsuit should be against the "ND State Board", and not the "NCAA". The only thing to give us hope, was when the judge asked the "NCAA" attorney, "with all the Chippewa tribes, you only required one tribeʼs approval over the objections of others, and with the Seminoles, only one tribe was needed over the objections of the others" (looking at us he said) "arenʼt they Sioux enough", this came with about "5" minutes left for arguments. It was at that time I thought, what a "Sioux-per title" for my book!

NCAA Attorney Duncanʼs, presentation was basically, that the "NCAA" is a private organization, and doesnʼt have to follow certain federal laws. That there was never any intention of "intentional discriminating against Native Americans", or cause them any harm, when the "NCAA" adopted the policy, so the "NCAA" is not guilty of discrimination. That, the Settlement/Agreement was between the "University" and the "NCAA" therefore the Sioux have "NO STANDING". When questioned by the judge about the "Notre Dame Fighting Irish", he responded with "no Leprechaunʼs" have complained! His sarcastic response makes clear to me at least, that "Native Americans are of no consequence to the NCAA", and are nothing but a "joke". The "NCAA" attorney stated the truth, "that the sanction were very minimal and ONLY applied to NCAA sponsored tournaments".

We left the court room down hearted, and feeling ambushed again. As we talked in front of the court house for a few minutes, we decided to go down the block to a small restaurant and tavern, and share our thoughts. We were all "shell shocked" at the first hour and twenty five minutes, and the judgeʼs apparent attitude, but we hung our hopes on the last five minutes. We did a good job of building our spirits up based on that one question, but deep down I think we all believed a decision had been made long before we even entered the court room, that day.

189

As Dave and I drove home, we expressed our disappointment that the issue of whether or not there is even a legitimate "NCAA policy" concerning Native Americans had been brought up. It was in our briefs to the court, but because of the judge's constant interrupting (on what we believed were unrelated subjects) of our attorney, the subject never had a chance to be brought up. I don't know if that was intentional or not, on the judge's part "but that the public would never hear the truth", we have our suspicions, as to the motivation on the part of the court.

The decision came out on May 2nd, 2012, and no surprise, it was just as we suspected "in favor of the NCAA'. (I personally don't know why the court ruling took so long, other than maybe for appearance sake). Our take on what the judge said "The NCAA is a private organization, and does not have to follow Federal Law, and that Indians have no standing". The judge's decision gives some cover to dismiss the case, and save the "NCAA Executive Committee, ND State board, Attorney General, and the University", and also, keep the public in the dark.

This is my interpretation of the ruling. "The NCAA is a private organization, and is free to do anything they want, to anybody they want, and the law be damned", as judges can always find precedence to justify any political ruling they wish. As for the claim of discrimination, "their only Indians, No rights exist". History has clearly shown that we are of no value. Therefore, he dismisses this lawsuit. They have no rights so how can they have "Standing"?

For everybody's information, I have to report, that this same Federal Judge (Ralph Erickson), had another case before him, at the same time as ours, 6 UND Native students and members of B.R.I.D.G.E.S (only two of them actually had a little Sioux blood) brought a lawsuit against the Governor and legislators for discrimination, when passing the law declaring UND well be known as the Fighting Sioux. These were two different lawsuits at the same time; 180 degrees apart, and this judge heard them both, and ruled the same in each, at almost the same time. Indians have no standing (Again, this is my belief; you make up your own mind).

But life goes on, and we still had the June State wide primary vote to get done. Because of lack of funds, the only campaign we could put

SAVE THE NAME...SUPPORTERS OF UND FIGHTING SIOUX
NICKNAME AND LOGO. LEFT TO RIGHT: PAM BREKKE,
REED SODERSTROM, AND EUNICE DAVIDSON; STOPPED IN
KENMARE MAY 23RD AS THEY TRAVELED THE STATE TO CONVINCE
RESIDENTS TO VOTE "NO" ON MEASURE 4.

on was personal appearances at petition signings. We crisscrossed the state, one weekend we'd be in Fargo, the next in Bismarck, than to Minot, Williston, and Dickenson out west. We were in Grand Forks, and to Grafton.

Much of the expense came from our personal pockets, which were running low. We hit the four corners of the state, and everything in between. We were on the Turtle Mountain Chippewa reservation, and were joined by the very artist who did the magnificent symbol, or (logo). Although, we didn't meet every member of the tribe, we did talk too many, and the tribal news reporter came out to interview us. We were set up at a gas station convenient store which served as almost a community center. Of all that came our way, only one individual opposed the name and symbol (as Bennett Brien the artist points out) IT IS NOT A LOGO, he said. He said; everything in the drawing has meaning. But even the person opposing the name and image, once shown the proof of what we had been going through, signed the petition in protest of those in power, (who he felt are racist).

Everywhere we went we were treated well. We were at Rib Fest, Car shows, even the State events, and at every event that the "State or University" was involved with; they always tried to deny us access.

But as we traveled around the state, it was clear that the deceitful, and distortion tactics put out by the opposition were taking a toll.

After our referendum petitions had been officially accepted on February 7, 2012, by the state, the "UND Administration, and Alumni Association" went into full gear. They reported; they were going to spend a quarter of a million dollars on an ad campaign. We were told that they spent almost a million dollars on it, though. Our measly seven thousand dollars could not come close to competing with them, and our personal pockets were being pulled inside out.

One of their most powerful TV ads, was a total distortion of "NCAA sanctions" it showed a UND hockey player skating on to the ice, only to have the lights shut off. This ad, played on all the state TV stations, and it strongly suggested, if we keep the name and image, UND could and probably would lose all its sports teams. The name must go, if you want the lights to stay on.

They reported statements by the "President of the Big Sky", but down played, or failed to mention that those statements always said; may happen or could happen, but he never said "would" happen.

Even, during one of the televised hockey games at the Ralph Engelstad arena, "UND athletic director Brian Fasion", while being interviewed between hockey periods, talked about how the sanctions were going to "Kill UND" sports if the name stays. Four things wrong about this: First issue; it is a violation of State Law, for any individuals connected to "State Funded Organizations" to lobby for, or against any ballot initiative, Second issue; it is a false claim, the sanction could only be enforced "in NCAA tournaments", and that the name and image could not be displayed; Third issue; this was done inside the "REA", which we had been denied, even outside access too, through the court: Fourth issue; Fasion stated, "that in a recent teleconference with athletic directors of the Big Sky conference the name and image was of big concern", but, in that conference call, there was no mention of the issue, and Fasion, was forced to admit it later. Clearly his

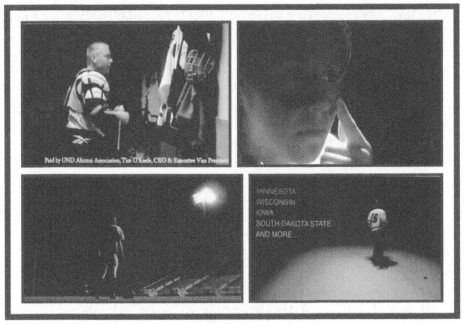

TYPES OF ADS PUT ON THE AIR BY THE ALUMNI ASSOCIATION
TO PROMOTE RETIREMENT...ALL DISTORTIONS

access to the arena was a double standard. We did complain to Jody Hodgson, and I don't think it happened again.

Forum Communications, which owns most of the news outlets "Newspapers, TV, and radio" in the state continually published, and broadcast forecast of gloom and doom, through their outlets. They cherry picked sentences out of full statements to print that gave a distorted vision to the reader, or listener. Such as "Doug Fullerton, President Big Sky Conference" statements that the name "may" become an issue in the future, but after their editing, the reader was left with the impression that we would not even get into the "Big Sky conference", when in fact we had joined in 2010, and had all games scheduled through the 2015, season. UND was, and is officially a member of the Big Sky, with a legal contract.

In the month leading up to the June primary vote, the "Alumni Association" stepped up their campaign, and saturated the air waves, with the distortion (lies), and everywhere we went, people were saying "if not for the sanctions we would vote to keep the name and logo, but the sanctions will kill UND". The citizens were told, of how Minnesota, and Wisconsin said, " they would not play UND if the

193

name stays", but they were never told, that both had already joined the "Big 10", and would not be playing UND anyway, regardless of the name.

We heard of how the "UND Alumni Association" spent upwards of a quarter of a million dollars in an ad campaign, although they said; only that quarter of a million would be spent. It shouldn't cost a quarter of a million to just lie, but to get them on TV it would, just more of my thoughts.

Those, who took the time, to allow us to inform them of the truth, and show the proof to back up what we claimed, they said; "they would be voting to keep the name and image, and were horrified to learn just what was being perpetrated on them by these so called honorable people".

On June 7, 2012, just days before the vote, the "Alumni Association" chartered a plane from NDSU, and flew "Four UND coaches" around the state making four stops, to lobby against the name and logo. They flew from Fargo, to Bismarck, where they were informed that they were in "Violation of Campaign Laws" by using a "State funded University plane". The plane should have been grounded, and returned to Fargo at that point but no, they continued on to Minot, and spent the night. The next morning they continued on to Grand Forks, then back to Fargo. They knew they were "Violating State Law", but what the hell; it's only against Indians, so what is the damage? Even after they knew they were violating the law, they continued, "yeah, some role models", just my thoughts, again.

Another point about this; is that the "Coaches used their Credentials of being a coach at UND", to bolster their importance. As individuals, they are perfectly authorized to state their views on the subject at their own personal expense. The law says that they can say "my name is so-in-so" and I am opposed to the name and image for these reasons. But the law forbids the use of "I am so-in-so and I Coach at UND", and this is what will happen if the name stays. They brought the "University itself" into the debate, and they are "Forbidden under Law", to voice any views pro or con under State Law. But what the hell, it's only against Indians!

It has been reported that "President Kelly of UND" solicited the responses from the "Summit League, Big Sky, South Dakota State University, Iowa Hawkeye's, and NCAA". Much of "their full responses" were left out of any public reporting on those statements by "UND Administration or Alumni" press releases.

Now, a story that has gone un-reported; is that, a significant number of "Alumni" have cancelled their "support to the University", we also know of a number of residents within, as well as out of state who have cancelled their subscriptions to the "Grand Forks Herald", as well.

We have talked to a number of Alumni that are receiving letters from the University and Alumni Association, begging for any contributions even five dollars.

But the big day had arrived again. June 12th, 2012, and the polls were open. I can put it no other way, than our hopes were soundly defeated. The lies and distortions had won the day. It is worth noting; that just over "32" percent of eligible voters turned out for the primary and of that small margin, "67" percent voted to allow dropping the name. The vast majority of them did not vote in favor of dropping the name, as much as fear of the sanctions. If not, for the complete distortions of so-called sanction, there is little doubt, in my mind, that over 80 percent would have voted to keep the name and image.

In this battle of "7" years now, it was our only defeat at the hands of North Dakota citizens, and we cannot blame them for their decision. There is an old saying that is very fitting here "if you tell a lie enough times, people will come to believe it". In the "55,225" voters that stood with us, I'd say we talked to just about every one of them personally.

After the vote many said; they actually wanted to vote to keep the name, but were confused at the wording. "I think this was intentionally caused, because when it was first announced that the issue would be on the ballot, it was stated that a "yes" vote was to keep the name, and a "no" vote was to remove the name. Then it was changed to a "no" vote keeps the name, and a "yes" vote would allow the retirement. But

Statement from UND Alumni Association, Foundation Exec. VP CEO Tim O'Keefe

UND

"In the past I respected the core intentions of the Committee for Understanding & Respect, given our common affection for the Fighting Sioux name and traditions of the past.

That said, the people of North Dakota rightfully recognized the damage the University of North Dakota would incur by keeping the name, and on June 12 spoke in huge volume in support of UND.

Thus, any efforts in the future by those associated with the Committee for Respect & Understanding to create another referendum are not only ill-advised, they become malicious attempts to damage UND, its students, student-athletes and reputation.

It should be well understood the UND Alumni Association & Foundation will not stand idly and see its University damaged. Any attempt by the Committee for Understanding & Respect to do so will be met strongly, and we believe the voters in North Dakota will both resent and reject the Committee's efforts, and will respond with even greater support than on June 12.

The voters in North Dakota have spoken. The consequence over the last 45 days is a University of North Dakota more focused on its academic and athletic missions than I have seen in years. The UND Alumni Association & Foundation should be narrowly focused on the priorities necessary to take UND from great to exceptional, and this is where our intentions lie.

However, if we must waste time and effort to address this matter again, we believe our Board, management, and especially our constituents, will respond in even much stronger terms than we were forced to prior to the June 12 vote.

FROM THE DEVIL'S LAKE JOURNAL

even with that confusion, we had no illusions that we would have won. So now, it's time to regroup, and see just where we are at.

But now "Tim O'Keefe President of the Alumni Association" has actually threatens anybody who would be willing to continue to try and save the name and image. In a press release after the primary vote held on June 12th, 2012, he names our committee by name, and warns us to drop it or else.

CHAPTER 18:
THE CONCLUSION AND SOME OF
MY THOUGHTS AND OPINIONS

In the mid 1990's, as I was visiting more with my Grandmother Alvina Albert's, she asked two things of me to do in my lifetime just as she had done. She said; *"no matter what, don't ever sell your land, without our lands we have nothing"*, and she said *"always keep good relations with the University of North Dakota", "* we elders have worked hard at establishing many Native American programs there", she said; *"years ago our people hunted Tatanka (Buffalo) for survival now we have to get educated for our survival.* Education is where it's at, that is our Maza'ska (money) to provide for our families now.

Wisdom comes from experience. Education teaches us about past experiences and it's the pathway to wisdom. My elders had great wisdom and they shared that with us. My Grandmother demonstrated that spirit that was connected to all our elders. Education is the path to a better understanding and a better way of life for our people. The gift that was given to the University of North Dakota (UND) has become a symbol of hope for our people. For 80 years, a tradition of Sioux Pride has been woven around that Symbol. It has bonded generations of peoples from all corners of life, to one name, our name... Sioux. My Grandmother's generation lived through extremely difficult times. They fought through cultural and traditional changes and yet survived. She was right, as is proven today; we cannot let them take away, what was given by our elders to all people.

Thinking on what my grandmother shared with me, and I have a lot of respect for her, and all our elders. In speaking with many of our tribal elders today, many have expressed those same sentiments over, and over again, how they support the University of North Dakota in using our likeness and name. The vast majority have always expressed that not only do they feel pride that such a University would choose to use our name and image, but the elders also knew of the educational values associated with it.

There have been many programs set up to help the Natives American Indians in education. UND, has lead the way for all institutions of higher education across the country, to create educational programs for Natives Americans. I was curious as to how many Sioux Natives have applied and received any scholarship awards at UND. I was especially interested in the Engelstad Sioux scholarship; I went to the University and asked if we could get a count of how many actual Sioux received the Sioux scholarship award. I was told, they could not give out any names or information on the scholarships. I didn't want any private information like, names or even the scholarship name, just an estimated figure of the actual Sioux at the University of North Dakota, but was told they could not give out that information. Like the sealed records from the lawsuit against the NCAA in 2006, I thought it might shed some light on what is really going on here, so I can only guess the reason, it must be hidden for just what it will tell?

It has been said by the Native American opposition, and printed in the press over, and over again, *"there are more important issues in Indian country!"* Hearing these comments, I've thought *"why have you been fighting so hard for many years to change the name and logo at the University of North Dakota if the issue is not that important* and *why have you worked so hard to silence the tribal member's voices?"*

Yes, there are many issues to take care of, that is what leaders are elected to do. Yet the leaders have chosen to disregard these issues, and focused on not allowing the members to have a say on this subject. Spirit Lake would not have had their voices heard, had we not formed the Committee to get a vote on this issue, and we all know how that turned out, and Archie and his committee on Standing Rock with the 1004 signatures on their petition, did they not have a right to be heard?

But to this day, nothing has taken place allowing tribal members to have their voice heard "on Standing Rock one way or the other".

The opposition is right; there are many other issues in Indian Country, but why have they not worked at solving those issues. We are a spiritually peaceful people, and we have not totally assimilated into the modern society, we have kept our culture and traditions. Instead, we are now adopting ways that are foreign to our Native Culture and Society. Instead, why do our leaders spend such an amount of energy and money on this issue, if the issue is not that important to them? Is it they don't like or support it, and must deny the tribal members a voice, because of what they might say. Another comment is; *"it causes racism"*, and I've thought to myself *"show me where and how it causes racism?"* for I have yet to see any. These are strong accusations, and they are cast without merit. These words are strong words spoken without backing. We must consider these words for what they are, words spoken from tongues who seek to divide, to cause strife and conflict. Again, this is not actions from men who are of the true Sioux culture and traditions.

I and many others have been asking other Native's around the State and Nation, especially at the University *"how do you feel about the Fighting Sioux name and logo"*? Overwhelmingly, the replies have been "it's a great name and symbol"! While some have said; *if it offends even "one" then maybe it's time to retire it?* I think to myself again, *"why does that one person's voice mean more than the majority which has shown eight out of ten Native Americans support for names and images"*. Then I thought about Jesse Taken Alive (one of the strongest opposition leaders) from Standing Rock in South Dakota, he opposes the name and logo, and he has stated; *"it causes discrimination and dehumanification"*, but why does his "Standing Rock School District" call themselves "The Wakpala Public High School, Fighting Sioux Althletics"? I question his motives and do not understand why he feels this way and is not fighting the fight there instead?

I discussed the professors, who testified at the "legislative hearings" on why they thought the Fighting Sioux name and logo should be retired. I heard the same claims from them; *"that it caused racism and discrimination"* and *"caused disruption in their classes and on the campus"*.

199

Shortly after the first hearing, I and my husband (Dave) went to the Chester Fritz (special collections), at the UND library, and while registering to get a library card, two students were helping with this; I asked them if they knew of Birgit Hans at Merrifield Hall, they both said, they took classes from her. I introduced myself, and asked them if they knew or heard of any interruptions in her classes, or others classes because of the Fighting Sioux name and logo? They both looked, somewhat surprised at the question and said "no". They both said, they wished the University would fight to keep the symbol and Sioux name. If these "so-called" acts are so strong and disruptive, why did they not come forth to the University administration, and bring those who are racists out in the open? There are so many stories that have been told about racism, and discrimination, supposedly over the name and logo, but when we investigated, we found no reports to security or for that matter any police reports, claiming the Fighting Sioux symbol and name were the cause of any problems, or an act of abuse caused by the name and symbol. What they are, are just stories from a fabricated political agenda to rid the Symbol from UND. We have to stand and challenge those who lay false claims. We have to challenge their words and accusations. My Grandmothers words ring even louder… "Education is the key." We must know the truth, and educate the citizens of this State on the truth behind retiring "80" years of tradition at UND. That is my purpose for picking up the pen and writing this book.

With the thousands of everyday citizens and alumni that have stood with us, and have become close "friends", the name maybe gone, but those friendships will last forever. I think to myself if the Fighting Sioux name can be taken away today, it can still be brought back tomorrow. In my history classes the instructors have asked *"why do we want and need to understand history?"* to understand history is so we don't keep repeating the mistakes from the past". If it was a mistake to take away 80 years of history that had become a tradition and had united so many cultures *"why let it slip away"?* I have to agree with Representative ReAnn Kelch when she asked Grant Shaft; *"why are you allowing this entity National Collegiate Athletic Assocation (NCAA) to come into our state and tell us what to do"?* For all that was needed (if they really wanted to keep it), was for the ND State Board of Higher Education and the University of North Dakota officials to stand with the Spirit Lake Tribe, and tell the

(NCAA) to back off or else! It had been done before by the, "Saginaw Chippewa Tribe of Michigan".

All they had to do, was research the other eight Universities that had been granted exemption with approval of one tribe in their state, and in the case of Catawba College in North Carolina, they received approval from a tribe from a different State, "South Carolina". I believe, UND would have been exempted from NCAA sanctions, if the University would have stood tall. Furthermore, since how and when does the NCAA have so much power to tell the State funded Universities in the United States, who can and cannot use images from many cultures? The NCAA's sole purpose and how it came into existence, was to protect college athletes from injury and abuse on the collegiate field, nothing more. And, look what it has become today.

It is my firm opinion that "none of this "turmoil" would have happened, if only as Mr. Burggraf said *"we had leaders such as Tom Clifford or Ralph Engalstad at the helm"* But sadly, we did not. Instead outsiders were brought in (my opinion) to scuttle any attempts to save the name and image.

But I would like to end on positives.

With all the negatives stories flooding the media, there has also been many, many, many, positives to come out of this that have gone unreported.

The biggest positive, is that most North Dakotans don't blame the Sioux for the name change anymore, and just how "many non-Native stood with us in this fight, and put themselves out there to be ridiculed by the powers that be". This demonstrates the spirit of what our elders knew of. The blending of people of all walks of life, to a common bond that brings people together, not tearing them apart, not fighting, but in harmony, not quarreling, but standing together, living together. We are all connected. The Fighting Sioux Symbol has been blessed by men of strong spiritual grounding, with wisdom, and foresight. This gift has healed the wrongs of past generations, and has done more positive, than any negative stone that might be raised in attempt to deface any positive. We are from a great State. We walk on the same earth that many generations have done before us. This is Dakota

Territory, and now carries the name of North Dakota. It is Sioux and we Sioux share that name with all people. As the UND student body so proudly hails at the end of the National Anthem, "and the home of the ....SIOUX!" That is priceless. All Sioux people should be proud to hear their name spoken. For a good name, is only good, as long as it comes off the lips of men. When it is no longer spoken, it will have gone into obscurity, gone forever.

There is a better understanding by non-natives as to just who we Dakota (Sioux) are, and our culture. They know the majority's voice has been silenced, and we have their respect, for we did not stoop to the underhanded tactics of the opposition.

The North Dakota Legislators did stand with the Sioux for a brief time, and although it was brief, I don't know if this ever happened before in the Nation.

A movement has begun uniting Natives as well as non-Natives, to stop the onslaught against Native Pride. We have talked to people from Boston to San Diego, from Portland to the Carolina's, from North Dakota to Texas, mostly Native American's, but also non-Natives and we all agree "the attacks most stop" and we hope to work on that by educating people on who we are.

More and more of our young people are awaking to the pride in which they are as Native Americans Indians, and expressing that pride with the help of Fighting Sioux apparel.

The professors at our Universities that are trying to teach you what to think, rather than how to think, are now being exposed for just who they really are.

UND Fighting Sioux may have been sidelined, but it is not forgotten, as can be seen with all the Fighting Sioux apparel worn at UND sporting events.

I have been moved to change the direction of my education to focusing on to true Dakota history and wanting to teach that history "not to foster hate, but understanding". We are not now or ever have been helpless victims. Education of our rich history needs to be accurately told in the classroom. Our institutions need real teachers of

202

history who know the past and can bring that knowledge to the classroom, and have a strong message that helps us all understand our pasts. Who we are, and where we came from. Right or wrong, the past is the past, but we must teach our children accurately for they will be doomed to repeat our past mistakes. As in Dakota culture, we must look 7 generations ahead for our children on our decisions we make today, for they are the ones, who will pay the price for our actions today. We must seek counsel and employ wisdom from our past, in our actions today.

I know, I and my Tribe will survive and the attacks on us in the media, and others have only made us stronger and more united.

I cannot end without stating the historical facts as to "history repeats itself".

From the 1830's to 1860's in what was to become the State of Minnesota, a small but powerful group of individuals (trading post owners, politicians, Indian agents, and land speculators) worked very hard to bring about hostilities to break out with the true owners of the territory "The Dakota Sioux" and because of the deceit, distortions, lies, outright theft and humiliation, they perpetrated on the Dakota people, in 1862 they had accomplished their desire and war broke out. We Dakota were of no more use or benefit to them, except for what monies we still had coming to us. With the war they caused and the help of a misguided US Government (who was also lied to) the Dakota, out gunned out manned were removed from our homeland in Minnesota and the monies we were still owed filled the pockets of that small but powerful group to the brim with what was ours. Many whites tried in vain to help the Dakota and were labeled out cast by the biased media and ridiculed. (One such story is "Six Weeks in the Sioux Tepees, by Sarah Wakefield)

Today we find the same story. From 1930 to 1980 the Sioux name helped bring a small University out of the shadows to a much respected University on a national platform. Then in the 1980's till today, a small but powerful group through deceit, distortions, outright lies, and deception have brought about the removal of our name and image. We are of no further use or benefit to this small but powerful group of individuals and with the help of a biased media, powerful politicians to promote their deceit, distortions, and outright lies they

203

have accomplished their goal and desires by having removed us from view.

But just as history eventually tells the true story of Minnesota Territory and how Henry Sibley a Minnesota politician and trading post owner facing bankruptcy in 1851 received more than a fourth of what was <u>obligated to be paid to the Dakota Sioux in 1852</u> from the Treaties of Traverse De Sioux and Mendota. The theft of $149,000.00 saved his butt. Then there is Governor Ramsey who made much of his vast wealth from his real estate business in Minnesota and violated the very treaty he was responsible for in 1851, or Senator Rice from Minnesota who was also in real estate and help persuade the US Government to turn on the Dakota in 1862 through deceit, deception, and outright lies and what about US Government Indian Agent Joseph R. Brown, who received $39,000.00 of Dakota monies as a trading post owner in 1852 also. The Dakota Chiefs and Full Bloods received nothing for their lands in Minnesota and Iowa. Because of their written communications and investigations the truth will always appear. (Source, 33rd Congress 1st Session "report of the Commissioners" Investigation of Alexander Ramsey for Fraud and Misconduct") and (Congressional Globe 1833 to 1870).

The same will happen to this small but powerful group here in North Dakota. The answers to questions such as "why did the Attorney General recommend signing the Settlement/Agreement in 2007 when it put North Dakota in a worse position and guaranteed losing, or why did the Chancellor talk about early retirement early in 2008 when the Tribal members are working to fulfil the Settlement, and why was an outsider the only name given by the Chancellor for UND's new President, why did the North Dakota State Board of Higher Education (SBHE) only work with the opposition? These questions and more will eventually be answered.

My book has only told what happened and at this point we can only wonder why this did happen. But as history has shown "the truth will eventually be told" and I can only hope it does not take a hundred years as with my ancestors.

I leave you with these closing thoughts.   Why was the Sioux name given to UND by the elders of the Dakota people?   What has that name brought to the people of North Dakota? Do you think

204

UND benefactor Ralph Englestad would have built the building and design it the way he did, if he knew that the current stewards of this institution would bow to those who seek to destroy what UND is as the Fighting Sioux?   In a nation of laws where individuals are given protections by our founding documents, we Sioux, as dual- citizens of this nation, are afforded the same rights as any other citizen of this country, and in those rights, we find our rights to our religious freedoms and our rights to be heard, by majority.   Why have we been silenced? Why have we not been heard? Why have we not been invited to the debate?

Aren't we Sioux enough?

Like us on Facebook "Aren't We Sioux Enough"?

CHAPTER 19:
THEY JUST WON'T LET IT GO

"Less than 150 years have gone by since the battle of The Little Big Horn. We are so close to history, just a blink in time. And "how soon we forget" how bravely our forefathers fought for their families and beliefs. Nothing since then has been done to bring some sense of honor, dignity and normality to Indian country. Now another similar crisis and so you face a new challenge. Just as the Jews today raise money to build new synagogues, so no one will ever forget the holocaust. So the "Fighting Sioux" name and logo, plus the North Dakota hockey rink that honors all Native Americans should stand forever so that no one will ever forget the genocide that was perpetuated to the Native Americans by the US government."

Bill LeCaine
Former UND Sioux and
Pittsburgh Penguins Hockey Player

We would encourage readers to read the NCAA Constitution and Manual, then read the minutes from the January 2008 NCAA Convention. They can be found online simply by Googling "NCAA Manual and NCAA Convention, January 13, 2008". We believe the NCAA Executive Committee did not and does not have the authority to adopt their so-called policy on Native American names and imagery, as was stated in North Dakota's original 2006 lawsuit and according to the ND "Attorney General", the NCAA recognized it also. We further believe: the 2008 NCAA Convention did not give the

NCAA Executive Committee the power to adopt a policy that violates the NCAA Constitution. Pay particular attention to the response to Todd Hutton (Utica College) when he requested an example of what the proposed amendment would cover (NCAA Convention 2008).

Now for something new: just before finalizing our book for publishing, on April 10th, 2014, another event has taken place that needs mentioning. Although the opposition has won the war, they still are not satisfied. It appears that, not only must we be removed from view, we must also be totally forgotten. Just as basketball has the Final Four, hockey has the Frozen Four, and the University of North Dakota had made it there. Just as every other University shows signs of support for their team, so did UND students and the Sororities on campus.

A sorority on campus hung a banner to support our team in the Frozen Four, only to be chastised by the UND Administration, NCAA, and Native American Center. **No Where on It**, is the logo or Fighting Sioux to be found, so what's the complaint?

From the fevered pitch, by the media, you would have thought a major earthquake, or something of that sort had happened. It brought out every so-called "Racist" expert, out, to be on the talk-Radio around the State. It was even said by one so-called expert; "anyone who supports names and images, must be a racist". I guess that would have included us Native Americans who support Native "names and images" as well. In truth, if the press would not have exploited the story, no one would have ever known it happened.

It went so far as the sorority having to take the banner down and now a number of the sorority members have been required to take "sensitivity training", by orders from the University President and that's not all. A man from North Dakota was visiting in Harrisburg, Pennsylvania and was invited to join friends in their suite at the Philadelphia Arena, where the Frozen Four was being played. They hung a Fighting Sioux Flag "inside" their box at the arena, only to be told to remove it by security guards, apparently on orders coming from the NCAA and the University. For those of you who may have watched the National televised game with Minnesota on April 10, 2014, you may have noticed the Flag early in the first period and

207

SORORITY BANNER

wondered why it was never shown again or you may have seen the fans with Fighting Sioux apparel on, early in the first period and wondered where they went. They were still there, but the cameras could not show them.

The hurt, anger, pain, and remorse that many North Dakotans feel over the deceitful theft of our pride, is of no meaning? Where is the sensitivity towards us, and 80 years of tradition? Now we are told, we can't even remember, what use to be. The Honor and Tradition of "80" years of pride, must be no more; it must be totally eliminated from history.

We made a request of the University on April 1, 2014, to use a part of the logo on the cover of our book. They asked to see it, and then denied us any use, of any part of the logo, on April 14, 2014. Attorneys have told us that, the University would probably lose in court, but could and probable would tie the book up for a couple of years in court.

My thought was: where is a required "sensitivity training" for the UND Administration, ND SBHE and NCAA: if anyone needs sensitivity training, it is the UND Administration, ND SBHE, and the NCAA, for it is "they" , that have shown nothing but disrespect for Indians, especially the Sioux. They have fought the North Dakota Sioux at every step, since 2006. They have no legitimate or moral right to suggest anyone needs "sensitivity training".

These people do more harm to Native Americans, than any name or image could ever do. They believe, "Free Speech" will be tolerated, only when what it says happens to be something the powerful agree with. Any reminders of true history must be eliminated, unless it helps this group of elites. Pride is something, only they have a right to and their treachery must be kept hidden, so as not to reveal their true agenda, whatever that may be.

In another somewhat related story from April 15, 2014:

U., Ute Tribe reach agreement on continued use of Utes

"Little Miss Ute Tribe Sundae Pargeets watches as University of Utah President David Pershing, center, and Ute Tribe Chairman Gordon Howell, right, finish signing a memorandum of understanding Tuesday, April 15, 2014, between the tribe and the school. The new agreement allows University of Utah sports teams to continue using the Ute name and the drum and feather logo. In exchange, the university will provide scholarships for Native American students, create an unpaid part-time position to advise Pershing on Native American affairs and its athletes will take part in outreach events with Native American children". (Courtesy of Geoff Liesik, and Desert News, Salt Lake City, Utah)

The difference between University of North Dakota and the University of Utah is called cooperation and mutual desire. I believe the picture published in the news article, with the Utes Tribal Chairman and University of Utah President, easily could have been

UND President Kelley and Spirit Lake Tribal leaders and "that" picture says a thousand words. But, sadly the UND Administration chose a different path.

Instead of working with the Tribe, they chose to work against the Tribe. Instead of honoring the past, they chose to destroy the past.

It must also be pointed out, although the format may have been different in 1969, honorable men got together and preformed a similar event as Utah. In the case of the University of North Dakota, the event was on a much grander scale. A Pow-Wow was held, that continued to this day and more importantly, a Sacred Pipe was used by, Spiritual Leaders, Elders, Vets, and Tribal Officials, giving the name eternally, and the many Native American educational opportunities began at UND, growing to the largest of any major University.

I believe: that a misguided handful of Native Americans, were just used to help get rid of the name and image. They were in fact, just used by the elites within the University System as a tool to accomplish "their personal goal" and all Native Americans will pay the consequences for these actions.

The recent complaints from the Native American Center, concerning, "funding cuts", is just a precursor to the future. Although the University will deny such consequences will take place, history shows that, efforts in past attempts to cut funding had failed. There is nothing standing in the way now.

THE FIGHTING SIOUX SPIRIT; A SPECIAL NOTE

There are so many fans of the Sioux name and logo it would be impossible to name everyone but one of my new friends who took the time to contact me during this time was a guy by the name of Brian Palmer. The reason I find him so awesome, he wanted to have a tattoo of the Sioux logo and have the "Fighting Sioux Forever" done in the Dakota Sioux language. I contacted a friend from Sioux Valley, Canada to make sure the spelling was right. The dedication this young man has is awesome; I have inserted his picture of his tattoo (with his approval) and another great picture that someone sent me in an email.

LEFT: "OHNIYE DAKOTA KICIZAPI" FIGHTING SIOUX FOREVER
RIGHT: A PHOTO EMAILED TO ME ANONYMOUSLY. WHAT A TRIBUTE
TO HAVE THE SIOUX FLAG ALONG WITH THE UNITED STATES AND NORTH
DAKOTA FLAGS.

REFERENCES

2013-2014 NCAA Division I Manual - JANUARY VERSION

NCAA policy Native names and images "NCAA Executive Committee issues guidelines" 2005

NCAA upholds ban on Fighting Sioux mascot Sports Bob Reha · Moorhead, Minn. · Apr 28, 2006 Walter Harrison said the NCAA recently received three letters regarding UND's appeal. One was from a district representative on the Standing Rock Sioux Reservation. The letter cited support by tribal members for the Fighting Sioux nickname. The second was from the university president. Harrison says the third was from Standing Rock Tribal Chair Ron His Horse is Thunder.

State of North Dakota, by and through North Dakota State Board of Higher Education, and the University of North Dakota, Plaintiffs "District Court Grand Forks ND Nov 9, 2006, case # 06-C-1333"

NCAA lawsuit ND District Court Settlement/Agreement and Mutual Release October 26, 2007College Hockey: North Dakota, NCAA Reach Out-Of-Court Settlement In Nickname DisputeBy Patrick C. Miller • USCHO Arena Reporter • Oct. 26, 2007.Read more: http://www.uscho.com/2007/10/26/north-dakota-ncaa-reach-outofcourt-settlement-in-nickname-dispute/#ixzz2xOh38JaY Bernard Franklin, NCAA Senior Vice-President for Governance, Membership, Education and Research Services, said, "One fundamental purpose of the policy was and is to listen to the Native American community and the NCAA sought input from them during the settlement negotiations.

The settlement confirms that the Sioux people — and no one else — should decide whether and how their name should be used."

Friend-of-the-court brief-reporters committee for freedom of information case # (18-06-C-1333 Nov. 20, 2007)

NCAA Publications - *2008 NCAA Convention* Proceedings*www.ncaapublications.com/p-3870-2008-ncaa-convention-proceedings....*DescriptionProceedings and information from the 102nd *NCAA* Annual *Convention* held January 10-14, *2008* in Nashville, Tennessee.

North Dakota State Board of Higher Education minutes (ND SBHE Minutes, February 4, 2008, May 14, 2009)

Grand Forks Herald "Archives Section "Fighting Sioux", Grant Shaft, and Chancellor Goetz, 2007 to 2012"

Tu-Uyen Tran City Beat "Grand Forks city beat city hall, UND and other stuff" (UND nickname debate comes to nickname committee February 26, 2009)

WDAZ-TV (April 16, 2009)

District Court, Ramsey County, North Dakota November 9, 2009 (Committee for Understanding and Respect vs State of North Dakota, by and through the ND SHHE case # 09-C-00419)

North Dakota Supreme Court, March 23, 2010 (case # 20100022)

2011 House Education Committee Hearing Bill **HB 1263**

Page 1 Page 2 *2011 HOUSE* STANDING *COMMITTEE* MINUTES ...*www.legis.nd.gov/...2011/.../hb1263....*North Dakota Legislative Assembly Jan 26, 2011 - *House Education Committee. HB 1263*. 01/26/11. Page 2. Rep. ... this *bill*. This deserves to have a *hearing*. Chairman RaeAnn Kelsch: ...

United States District Court for The District of North Dakota Northeastern Division case No. 2:11-cv-95

2011 Special Session House Standing Committee Minutes (House Education Committee, Pioneer Room, State Capital" SB 2370, 11-7-2011 Jobs #16940"

United States Court of Appeal for the Eighth Circuit "Appeal No. 12-2292

ARTICLE NOTES:

Chapter 14, Page 148

Former UND hockey player sends Faison scathing e-mail for testifying against nickname bill at capitol

Frank Burggraf, who played on two UND national championship hockey teams in the early 1980s, sent a long, scorching e-mail last week to athletic director Brian Faison, denouncing him for testifying against the Fighting Sioux nickname bill at the Legislature.

By: **Chuck Haga**, Grand Forks Herald

Frank Burggraf, who played on two UND national championship hockey teams in the early 1980s, sent a long, scorching e-mail last week to athletic director Brian Faison, denouncing him for testifying against the Fighting Sioux nickname bill at the Legislature.

Burggraf shared the e-mail with other former Sioux athletes, who in turn have passed it along to countless other partisans of the nickname and logo, much as happened with a mass email UND hockey coach Dave Hakstol sent out urging support for the nickname preservation bill then before the state Senate.

The Senate voted to approve the bill, which directs UND to keep the Fighting Sioux name and logo, and Gov. Jack Dalrymple signed it. Faison had testified against the bill when it was heard by a Senate committee.

"To say that I am furious is an understatement," Burggraf wrote in his email. "You are supposedly a steward of the rich tradition that Fighting Sioux athletics represents in the hearts and souls of all those who embrace the university. You were given the trust of carrying that tradition when you accepted the AD position. You were not employed to change it.

"You fumbled the ball on your first carry in the critical game for Sioux athletics. You are doing more harm than good and, like in sports, your individual performance is detrimental to the team and you should be benched."

Faison said on Wednesday that he received the e-mail and responded to it, acknowledging "the depth of his feeling" and suggesting they get together to talk when the season is over.

"He certainly has his feelings and has the right to express them," Faison said. "Beyond that, I can't comment."

Testifying before the Senate Education Committee, Faison said the nickname bill poses "competition and scheduling" problems for the university, including scheduling difficulties "driven by schools that won't play us" because of the continuing nickname saga.

"So, it's out there," Faison said, referring to concerns that passage could jeopardize all aspects of UND's athletics programs, including its advance to Division I. "It's real," he said. "It's legitimate."

'Sacred ground'

Burggraf, 50, played hockey at Roseau (Minn.) High School before suiting up for UND from 1978 to 1982. He was a member of the 1980 and 1982 national championship teams and the 1979 team that reached the NCAA final but lost.

Now a pilot for Delta Airlines, living in Fargo but flying out of Minneapolis, he also conducts a hockey skating school and business in Fargo.

In an interview Wednesday, he said he has heard from many former Sioux athletes, "a lot of football and basketball and other guys" as well as former hockey players "from my time, before my time and after my time," who seconded the sentiments he expressed in his letter.

215

"We all come together under this," he said. "This is sacred ground for us."

He also praised Hakstol for his in-character "ferocious" defense of the Fighting Sioux tradition and predicted more alumni — athletes and others — are prepared to rally under that banner.

"He has a huge shadow of alumni who will come forward," Burggraf said. "He's not standing alone."

In his e-mail, sent Friday, Burggraf told Faison that he needed "to express to you my frustration, irritation and disgust with your testimony against the use of the Fighting Sioux nickname. … I find your testimony in favor of retiring the nickname unacceptable behavior for our 'Athletic Director.' "

The primary duty of someone in that position "is to represent the rich tradition that has been chiseled out of the land that once was the home of the Sioux Nation," he wrote.

He asked Faison to provide proof that the name and logo are "harmful, degrading (or) a poor representation" of the Sioux people.

And he asked, "Are you (and President Robert Kelley) prepared to pick up the economic tab that you are about to lose if you are successful at retiring the use of the nickname? I doubt it."

Burggraf wrote that he has heard Faison and others "say it is time to move on," and he agrees.

"You and those who have come to change UND, it is time for you all to move on and get off the campus. As a taxpayer and a 25-year North Dakota resident, I resent those of you who step onto the campus of the university and yield or cower to the minority for the sake of peace or being politically correct.

"You have shown your true colors by your testimony. They are not true Green and White. You have chosen the wrong side. You might as well have put on a Gopher jersey or cheer for NDSU. If President (Thomas) Clifford were on campus today, you would be looking for a new job."

Made in the USA
Monee, IL
20 July 2021

73610374R00125